Sharing Responsibility in Shaping the Future

Edited by
Brigid Reynolds, s.m.
Seán Healy, s.m.a.

Social Justice Ireland

I.S.B.N. No: 978 1 907501 05 0
First Published: September 2011

Published by:
Social Justice Ireland
Working to build a just society

Social Justice Ireland
Arena House
Arena Road
Sandyford
Dublin 18
Ireland

Tel: 01-213 0724
e-mail: secretary@socialjustice.ie
website: www.socialjustice.ie

Sponsored by

AIB Investment Managers
AIB Investment House,
Percy Place,
Dublin 4.
Tel: (01) 661 7077
Fax: (01) 661 7038

TABLE OF CONTENTS

	Introduction	v
1.	**The Council of Europe's proposed new Charter on Shared Social Responsibilities** Addressed at conference by Gilda Farrell	1
2.	**Shared Social Responsibility as a Key Concept in Managing the Current *Interregnum*** Mark Davis	28
3.	**Sharing Social Responsibility in Shaping the Future: A Trade Union Perspective** David Begg	55
4.	**Sharing Responsibility in Building the Future: A Business Perspective.** Danny McCoy	72
5.	**Intergenerational Solidarity and its Role in Shaping the Future** Mary Cunningham	79
6.	**Sharing Responsibility in Shaping the Future: An Environmental Perspective Participatory Democracy - The Story of a Trojan Horse** Michael Ewing	84
7.	**Sharing Responsibility to Maximize Positive Outcomes: Co-Production, Community Participation and Public Services** Ivan Cooper	103
8.	**Sharing Responsibility for Shaping the Future - Why and How?** Seán Healy and Brigid Reynolds	134

CONTRIBUTORS

David Begg is General Secretary of the Irish Congress of Trade Unions (ICTU)

Ivan Cooper is Director of Advocacy at The Wheel

Mary Cunningham is CEO of the National Youth Council of Ireland (NYCI)

Mark Davis Director of the Bauman Institute, University of Leeds

Michael Ewing is Coordinator of the Irish Environmental Network (IEN)

Gilda Farrell is Head of Social Cohesion Research and Development Division, Council of Europe

Seán Healy is Director, Social Justice Ireland

Danny McCoy is Director General of the Irish Business and Employers Confederation (IBEC)

Brigid Reynolds is Director, Social Justice Ireland

INTRODUCTION

In recent decades intellectual and political elites have paid little attention to issues concerning the future. Those who raised questions concerning the future, what it might look like, how it should be shaped and who should play a part in deciding its shape were dismissed as being out of touch with the 'real' world. It was regularly pointed out to such questioners that the market would make these decisions and there wasn't much point in wasting time 'theorising' about such issues. Media coverage of events and discussions concerning issues rarely focused on the future and what its shape might be. The so-called 'experts' who were consulted, who appeared on TV and radio programmes and wrote extensively in newspapers were mostly economists. It seemed that everything could be reduced to its economic dimensions and only economists had a useful contribution to make to the discussion and problem-solving. The crises of recent years have highlighted the paucity of this approach.

Since 2007 the world's economy has been in turmoil. The world's political structures have failed to deal with this turmoil in a fair and just manner. Yet the failure for the most part to address the future in anything more than economic and fiscal terms displays a profound lack of awareness of the issues at stake. Of course the economic issues are very important but so are the political, the cultural, the social and the environmental. There is an urgent need for discussion of the vision of the future that is guiding decision-making across the board.

This publication addresses the issue of sharing responsibility in shaping the future and how this might be achieved. Questions concerning responsibility have been widely debated in recent times. Among these are questions on why ordinary people who had no part in the decisions made by banks and other institutions that caused the current series of crises, are now being forced to take responsibility for the consequences of dangerous and sometimes illegal activities of those who played a central role?

The issue of responsibility goes even further. Following on from recent crises people's rights are at risk as are social protection, the welfare state and democracy itself. This situation is exacerbated by many other challenges facing the world today ranging from pandemics to environmental devastation, from nuclear annihilation to mass migration of displaced people.

It is time that responsibility for shaping the future was shared in a meaningful way between all stakeholders in the interests of the common good. But sharing responsibility raises its own series of questions such as:

- Why should responsibility be shared?
- How can responsibility be shared in a real and meaningful manner at local, national and international levels?
- How can people ensure their voice is really heard or that future generations are protected?

The chapters in this book, which were first presented at a policy conference on the topic of *Sharing Responsibility in Shaping the Future*, seek to address some of the key questions and issues that emerge in this context.

This publication is the 23rd volume in this series organised and published by *Social Justice Ireland* (previously published by *CORI Justice*) which has sought to address these questions and issues on a day to day basis. It includes a working draft of the *Charter on Shared Social Responsibilities* being prepared by the Council of Europe.

Social Justice Ireland is concerned with issues of principles, paradigms and guiding values as well as with the specifics of problems and policies. It approaches all of these from a social justice perspective. *Social Justice Ireland* is a recognised social partner within the Community and Voluntary pillar of social partners. In presenting this volume we do not attempt to cover all the questions that arise around this topic. This volume is offered as a contribution to the ongoing public debate around these and related issues.

Social Justice Ireland expresses its deep gratitude to the authors of the various chapters that follow. They contributed long hours and their obvious talent to preparing these chapters. A special word of thanks also to the AIB Investment Managers whose financial assistance made this publication possible.

Brigid Reynolds
Seán Healy
September 14, 2011

1.

Draft text of the Council of Europe's Charter on shared social responsibilities

The Council of Europe has been preparing a Charter on shared social responsibilities.

This is the draft of that Charter which will be voted on later in 2011.

Please note that it may change before receiving final approval.

The Committee of Ministers, under the terms of Article 15.b of the Statute of the Council of Europe

Considering that:

a. Europe, via the historical pathways specific to each country, seeks to secure equal access to fundamental rights, the ideal of universal social protection and a dignified life for all, enabling all individuals to freely develop their personality, retain control over their life, participate in societal choices and exercise their responsibilities towards their families, the community, the environment and future generations;

b. the people and institutions of Europe have acquired skills in the field of democratic citizenship, the welfare state, the rule of law, local self-government, social dialogue, partnerships and strategies for the political and non-violent resolution of conflicts and for developing frameworks and points of reference for harmonious co-existence; their knowledge and cultural heritages foster a critical and entrepreneurial spirit which is at the basis of institutional innovation, social experimentation and economic initiative;

c. in the current context, the democratic skills of the Europeans and their social and institutional achievements are faced with major social changes. In particular:

- the rise in inequalities, financial insecurity and poverty is combined with a global situation which casts doubt on the link between economic growth, job creation and sustainability, particularly in a context of increased competition for non-renewable natural resources, environmental limits and rapid climate change;

- migration towards Europe, and the presence of descendents of immigrants calling for full social and political recognition, requires European societies to ensure equal treatment, while at the same time incorporating cultural, religious and ethnic diversity into their practices;

- public over indebtedness, in a context of financial speculation, exposes states to the risks of repeated crises and weakens their ability to fulfil their role of ensuring access to social protection, health care, education, housing and common goods in general, even though equal access for all constitutes a fundamental source of confidence and social cohesion;

- the pressure of globalised markets on national institutions and local communities leads to fundamental decisions being taken which lack democratic control and which fail to meet the aspirations and hopes of the population;

- the lack of a comprehensive understanding of the impact of choices, including those relating to the private sphere, makes it difficult to implement a policy capable of preventing and overcoming the threats of irreversible environmental destruction;

d. faced with these challenges, the gap between politics and citizens, democratic deficits and the prevalence of short-term visions weaken the attachment felt for democratic institutions, increase the risks of violence and threaten social cohesion;

e. these changes, conveyed and amplified by the media, are directly reflected in European public opinion, which fluctuates between the search for a vision of the future and a feeling of uncertainty, unease and loss of confidence given the unpredictability of social changes and the limitations of the proposed alternatives to the status quo.

Convinced that:

a. in a context in which no-one is totally independent or immune from the damaging consequences of other people's actions or failure to act, the most advantaged population groups cannot ignore their interdependencies and responsibilities vis-à-vis the rest of society, particularly when the least advantaged see their achievements in terms of access to rights, public services and common goods placed under threat;

b. there is insufficient recognition of the unequal distribution of powers, resources and opportunities, bearing no relation to the allocation of social responsibilities, and inadequate steps are taken to rectify this situation, whether in decision-taking or in social and institutional arrangements, producing an unacceptable waste of human capacities and knowledge which are essential for collective progress;

c. at a time when the public sector is tending to reduce its role in the field of social policies and common goods, the other stakeholders do not always have the skills and motivation necessary to share social responsibilities in a context of interdependence;

d. the failure to take adequate account of the possible areas of complementarity between representative democracy, deliberative democracy and participatory democracy acts as a break on innovation in all fields in which the reciprocal nature of commitments and joint decision-making based on impartial reasoning are essential in order to guarantee the principles of social, environmental and intergenerational justice; to this end, it is imperative that individuals and social stakeholders are involved to a greater extent in the framing, implementation and evaluation of policies and measures having an impact in public life;

e. without renewed confidence in the possibility of inclusive societal progress, there is a danger that the exceptional legacy of the democratic values championed by the Council of Europe will be dissipated.

Resolved to:

a. gain an in-depth understanding of the nature of changes under way, so as to develop the collective skills to manage transitions and acquire a shared long-term vision in order to ensure that institutions and citizens are not paralysed by a feeling of powerlessness and fear or that power is not left solely in the hands of the strongest;

b. combat the causes of inequalities, poverty, insecurity and discrimination by developing and placing greater emphasis on a universal framework of inalienable and indivisible rights and common goods, as the basis of democratic citizenship which is inclusive of all forms of diversity;

c. reduce the gap between the formal recognition of rights and democratic principles (such as human dignity, equality, participation, social, environmental and intergenerational justice, harmonious co-existence in a plural society) and decisions and behaviour in practice which disregard or violate these rights and principles;

d. overcome the ideological barriers and inertia which make it difficult to link responsibilities and individual interests to approaches for joint action designed to secure social, environmental and intergenerational justice and acknowledging the value of reciprocity, solidarity and co-operation;

e. restore the ability of public institutions to rectify democratic deficits and to settle social and distributive conflicts by developing forms of dialogue based on the impartial search for the common good and mutual advantage, with the aim of establishing fair agreements and ensuring that the most vulnerable are fully recognised and protected from the harmful consequences of decisions in which they have had no part; and to support the steps taken by states to guarantee common goods;

f. promote the ability of companies to take account, in their strategies, of the interests of all stakeholders, both internal and external, and of the impact of their activity on society at large and drawing inspiration from the principles of the socially responsible and solidarity-based economy;

g. give greater acknowledgement and consideration to the contribution of the ethical and solidarity-based initiatives of citizens, non-governmental organisations, social enterprises, co-operatives and other forms of social networks to the preservation and creation of common goods and innovation in policies and public services;

h. broaden the choices available to citizens in pursuit of social, environmental and intergenerational justice, by providing them with relevant information and strengthening confidence in their capacity for initiative and in their creativity;

i. turn to account, in a globalised world, the advantages and values of the European model based on democracy, fundamental rights, recognition of human dignity and social cohesion;

Recalling that:

a. the Council of Europe's Revised Strategy for Social Cohesion, which defines the latter as the capacity of society to ensure the well-being of all its members, calls for the construction of a Europe of shared social responsibilities in order to achieve this goal, as one of its fundamental pillars;

b. the Social Cohesion Plan, launched by the Council of Europe in 2010, seeks to foster the involvement of citizens and players in defining priorities and responsibilities by means of deliberative democracy. The accession by territories taking part to a European Network of Territories of Co-Responsibility will reinforce their capacity to cooperate;

c. the European Union's 2020 Strategy calls for smart, sustainable and inclusive growth and sets among its chief objectives the reduction of poverty and a the efficiency in the use of resources, mainly fossil fuels, and that the European Platform against Poverty gives practical form to the aspirations of several groups of citizens and civil society organisations committed to constructing a more just Europe;

d. the enjoyment of the rights secured by the European Convention for the Protection of Human Rights and Fundamental Freedoms, the European Social Charter and the European Union's Charter of Fundamental Rights entails responsibilities and duties both between individuals and towards the human community at large, and to future generations, and consequently a European Charter on Shared Social Responsibilities is an indispensable complement to those instruments;

e. many recommendations approved by the Council of Europe's Parliamentary Assembly and Congress of Local and Regional Authorities support a change in the economic and social model based on the principles of democratic participation, social justice and sustainable development;

f. the Council of Europe already supports the establishment of a context conducive to the sharing of social responsibilities through the Convention on access to official documents, the Additional Protocol to the European Charter of Local Self-Government on the right to participate in the affairs of a local authority, the New Urban Charter and the Convention on the participation of foreigners in public life at local level;

g. the Aarhus Convention, which was adopted by the United Nations Economic Commission for Europe on 25 June 1998 and entered into force on 30 October 2001, recognises and protects citizens' rights to information, participation and access to justice in environmental matters; numerous international documents, such as the UNESCO Declaration on the responsibilities of the present generations towards future generations, the Earth Charter, the Manifesto on the future of the climate, the Manifesto on the future of food, the Aalborg Charter of European cities and towns towards sustainability and the Charter of Human Responsibilities recognise the need to preserve common goods and pass them on to future generations in a context of shared responsibility in the field of social and environmental justice;

h. the ISO 26 000 standard defines the societal responsibility of organisations by highlighting different core subjects which organisations should promote;

i. on 1 October 2009 the Council of Europe's Conference of International Non-governmental Organisations adopted a code of good practice for citizen participation in the decision-making process [CONF/PLE(2009)Code1];

j. numerous international projects underway supported by the OECD and the European Union, and the Council of Europe's activities on defining societal progress in co-operation with citizens and communities, are working on innovative ideas on the objectives of the prosperity and well-being of all, clarifying as well the shared responsibilities that this entails;

Recommends that the governments of member states:

1. alert all stakeholders to the risks of a regression in rights, social protection and democracy when faced with recurring crises and to the waste of citizens' human, intellectual and moral skills;

2. raise all stakeholders' awareness of reciprocity and mutual compliance with commitments in the establishment of rules, priorities and jointly decided action strategies;

3. encourage experimentation of a new approach based on the principle of shared social responsibilities, which seeks to link the decisions and action of the different players to the objectives of securing welfare and social, environmental and intergenerational justice, in a spirit of reciprocity, mutual accountability and a shared commitment to reducing social inequalities and inequalities of influence and to minimising the harmful consequences of unilateral decisions;

4. promote shared social responsibilities in order to nurture knowledge, skills and common strategies able to re-establish confidence in the future and the possibility of achieving progress in well-being for all, while taking the different interests into account in an impartial way, and assigning priority to the protection of fundamental rights and satisfying the needs required for a decent life;

5. encourage and legitimise new forms of deliberation, aimed at reducing inequalities of power and formulating preferences through reasoning and exchanges of views, using, in particular, the methods proposed by the Council of Europe in its work on social cohesion;

6. recognise and actively support the vital role played by local stakeholders, neighbourhoods, cities, towns, villages, cantons, districts and regions in constructing a Europe of shared social responsibilities;

7. help bring about new forms of co-operation and new structures of governance and use existing ones more efficiently, involving all

stakeholders and the various levels of responsibility and sectors of society, conducive to non-hierarchical and shared decision-making, including all current generations to ensure that political action is geared to the long-term, thereby avoiding a transfer of the risks and costs to the weakest groups or to future generations;

8. encourage renewed criteria for assessing initiatives in order to provide stakeholders with tools to ensure that the decisions taken are implemented in practice, and to verify the quality of results; to this end, promote the use of progress indicators taking into account the quality of life, freedoms and abilities, reductions in social disparities and in the risks of environmental damage;

9. ensure that learning processes, forms of participation, structures of governance and assessment criteria capitalise on the knowledge and contributions of all stakeholders in accordance with their abilities, roles and resources, paying particular attention to those who have less power, whose voices are less often heard, who have less legal protection and who suffer from the harmful consequences of other people's choices;

10. incorporate into public policies the lessons learned from experimental practices encouraging a sharing of social responsibilities, particularly in the field of combating the causes of poverty, inequality, and discrimination, the protection of common goods and the environment, the improvement of access to social protection and health-care systems and other public policies encouraging active citizenship through joint decision-making and co-production, sustainable choices regarding budgetary decisions, production, lifestyles and public and private investments and harmonious co-existence with due regard for plurality;

11. ensure that the Charter is widely disseminated among institutions, public authorities, companies, civil society organisations, trade unions, foundations, professional organisations, the media, social networks and citizens in general;

Instructs the Secretary General to transmit this recommendation:

a. to the political bodies of the Council of Europe;
b. to the European Commission, the European Parliament, the European Council, the European Economic and Social Committee and the Committee of the Regions;
c. to the national parliaments of member states;
d. to the international organisations.

Council of Europe Charter on Shared Social Responsibilities

Adopted under Committee of Ministers Recommendation CM/Rec. (2011) ....

Preamble

1. Considering that the aim of the Council of Europe is to achieve a greater unity between its members for the purpose of promoting the ideals and principles which are their common heritage, and safeguarding human dignity and the freedom and equality of everyone in Europe;

2. Committed to the principles laid down in the European Convention on Human Rights, the European Social Charter and the European Union's Charter of Fundamental Rights which stipulate that the enjoyment of rights entails responsibilities and duties both between individuals and towards the human community at large, and to future generations; considering that a European Charter on Shared Social Responsibilities is an indispensable complement to those instruments;

3. Concerned at the threat to the political and social achievements of Europe, linked to public over indebtedness, company relocations, climate change and the depletion of natural resources;

4. Considering that the succession of economic, financial and environmental crises affects people unequally, with the greatest effects being felt predominantly by the weakest and the least protected, even though they are not responsible for current imbalances;

5. Concerned at the growing gap between the formal recognition of rights and their implementation; considering that this gap fuels a sense of insecurity vis-à-vis the future, undermines legitimate confidence in democratic mechanisms and raises doubts about the ability of public and private institutions to improve living conditions, especially those of the less well-off;

6. Mindful of the risk of the resulting stigmatisation of those groups which can most easily be blamed without any real justification, such as the poor, migrants and minorities;

7. Concerned, in a context of interdependence, by the trend among states to reduce their role in key policies and services for collective well-being and by the continuing deterioration of economic conditions such as to prevent full employment;

8. Considering that these changes fundamentally alter the scope and substance of specific responsibilities, be they individual or collective, voluntary or statutory. Interdependence brings to the fore differences in values, conceptions of well-being and interests present in society. These differences can give rise to mutually destructive conflicts, to the waste of social, environmental and economic resources and to other negative externalities;

9. Considering that the gravity of the situation calls for new methods of governance, regulation, conflict management and redistribution incorporated into a long-term vision;

10. Convinced of the need, in order to generate confidence in the future, for social responsibilities to be shared equitably among public authorities, companies, civil society organisations, families and individuals.

11. Considering that in order to avoid friction, reduce imbalances of power and exploit the potential of mutual gains, it is essential to put in place co-operative solutions which can ensure for all stakeholders an equitable share of social and economic benefits.

12. Considering that such solutions will be possible provided that there is an impartial consideration of the different social demands, concepts of well-being and interests at stake, so as to identify common interests, while at the same time acknowledging the primacy of fundamental rights and the value of diversity. This consensual approach will enable European societies to pull together, generating solidarity imbued with the principles of social, environmental and intergenerational justice;

13. Confident that the sharing of social responsibilities is an alternative to the status quo which, through the involvement of all stakeholders, both strong and weak, will give rise to common and sustainable solutions, fully acknowledging their contributions and legitimate aspirations;

14. Convinced that Europe is the appropriate level for action to promote social cohesion, reduce inequalities and bring about social innovation, based on an interplay of skills between multiple stakeholders, sectors and tiers of authority;

15. Considering that the future of Europe and the preservation of its democratic and social achievements are closely linked to the ability of citizens and public and private institutions to understand the changes taking place and address the uncertainty generated by unprecedented interdependence between individuals, communities and organisations.

16. Wishing to stimulate a climate of confidence in the future, to strengthen democracy and develop the necessary social and moral resources to enable the citizens of Europe to act together to foster the universal protection of rights, the well-being of all, social cohesion, sustainable development and interaction between cultures, the Council of Europe proposes the implementation of the principle of shared social responsibility and agrees on the following:

Implementation of the present Charter:

1. Scope

Shared social responsibility does not replace specific responsibilities. Rather it complements and enhances them by encouraging social stakeholders and individuals to engage in transparency and to be accountable for their actions in a context of knowledge and decision-making constructed through dialogue and interaction. Nor does shared social responsibility entail assigning indiscriminately to the weakest players individual responsibility for their economic and social situation, but rather calls for a new approach to responsibility in a context of interdependence.

2: Definition of shared social responsibility

a. **responsibility** is defined as the state in which individuals and public and private institutions are required or are in a position to be accountable for the consequences of their actions or omissions in all fields of public and private life, with due regard for the applicable moral, social and legal rules or obligations;

b. **social responsibility** is defined as the state in which individuals and public and private institutions are required or are in a position to be accountable for the consequences of their actions or omissions in the fields of social welfare and the protection of human dignity, the environment and common goods, the fight against poverty and discrimination, and the pursuit of justice and social cohesion, showing democratic respect for diversity and for the applicable moral, social and legal rules or obligations;

c. **shared social responsibility** is defined as the state in which individuals and public and private institutions are required or are in a position to be accountable for the consequences of their actions or omissions, in the context of mutual commitments entered into by consensus, agreeing on reciprocal rights and obligations in the fields of social welfare and the protection of human dignity, the environment and common goods, the fight against poverty and discrimination, the pursuit of justice and social cohesion, showing democratic respect for diversity.

3. Definition of social, environmental and intergenerational justice

Shared social responsibility is a means of securing social, environmental and intergenerational justice.

a. Social justice is the guarantee of human rights, while meeting fundamental human needs, striving, through redistribution mechanisms, to reduce inequalities and securing collectively the conditions conducive to the development of the individual and his or her skills, regardless of gender, origins, race, beliefs or convictions;

b. environmental justice is the fair management of natural resources, the protection of common goods, the preservation of a healthy environment for all and, where appropriate, the reparation of or compensation for ecological damage. Under the principle of social justice, no group or individual should have to bear in a disproportionate way, the harmful consequences of damage to the environment;

c. intergenerational justice places future generations and their possibilities for development at the heart of present-day decisions, without their having to suffer the irreversible damage caused by the generations preceding them, while at the same time benefiting from what they have achieved. It is to be seen primarily in the preservation, enrichment and transmission of common goods and the frameworks of democracy and social protection for all. It presupposes dialogue among the present generations on the reduction of current inequalities in order to restore confidence in political processes which will result in social structures providing everyone with a level of security and control guaranteeing their autonomy.

4. Implementing conditions

The shared exercise of social responsibilities requires the following conditions to be in place:

a. No one shall be excluded from the decisions which have or may have significant and irreversible consequences for his or her existence and on the local or global political community in which he or she lives. Each individual or group of individuals must have the ability to take a decision or take part in an action having significant effects in the public arena. The public authorities, corporate bodies and individuals are urged to eliminate the legal, operational and material obstacles to the exercise of this right;

b. in particular, for their actions to be legitimately subject to the approval or disapproval of others, each individual or group of individuals must be able to have access to information on the impact of their actions, in order to foresee and verify their compliance with the norms of life in society;

c. there must be the broadest possible level of transparency in order to ensure that the information required for the sharing of social responsibilities is available to all the various stakeholders;

d. the principles, norms and priorities in the field of social, environmental and intergenerational justice must be the subject of broad debate and be agreed by democratic consensus having a significant influence on their substance and application;

e. these principles, norms and priorities must be able to create a feeling of solidarity and reciprocity between stakeholders, motivating them to action and to honouring their mutual commitments.

f. responsibility for acts cannot be regarded as shared between different individuals, institutions or bodies, if the latter have been unable to make any choice with regard to those acts.

5: Standards of action and decision
Policies based on the principle of shared social responsibility seek to

a. safeguard the social and political achievements of Europe and ensure their sustainability faced with the dangers of regression;

b. take account of the harmful consequences of decisions and actions in order to learn lessons from the mistakes of the past, to reduce as far as possible uncertainty and fear, injustice and unjustified discrimination, and to protect the rights of present and future generations;

c. encourage discussion and innovation in the field of welfare and social, environmental and intergenerational justice, based on new multi-stakeholder, multi-level and multi-sectoral institutional and organisational arrangements;

d. provide the weaker stakeholders with opportunities to influence decisions and priorities;

e. manage conflicts through the impartial mediation of interests and an understanding of the complexity of the issues at stake, while bearing in mind the principles of social, environmental and intergenerational justice;

f. build up everyone's confidence and ability to take action by giving them an opportunity to express their views on the objectives pursued, the means to be deployed and the criteria for assessing the strategies adopted;

g. adopt indicators making it possible to measure societal progress in terms of well-being for all, the reduction of disparities in living conditions and access to skills and common goods, the level of harmonious co-existence in a plural society and limitation of the harm caused to the environment.

6: Means of implementation

An effective strategy in the field of shared social responsibilities presupposes:

a. recognition of the full range of stakeholders, their demands and possible contributions in terms of action or suggestions, their rights and obligations, and their role in a social system based on close interdependencies;

b. deliberative processes, making it possible to refine the preferences of the stakeholders and establish priorities through exchanges of different arguments and viewpoints, and through the impartial arbitration of differing interests;

c. multi-stakeholder, multi-level and multi-sectoral innovation and skill and knowledge-acquisition processes making it possible for all involved to evaluate the consistency between the decisions taken and the European frames of reference in the field of fundamental rights, and paving the way for the equitable and democratic management of common goods;

d. forms of partnership and governance broadly involving the stakeholders at different levels and making it possible for a plurality of players to become involved and co-operate in a sustainable way;

e. institutional mechanisms offering confidence in the fact that each partner will act in accordance with the decisions taken and will refrain from any harmful behaviour or acting solely in his or her own interest to the detriment of the interests of others;

g. recognition of material and non-material common goods. Among the objects of rights, common goods are those which express a functional utility for the exercise of fundamental rights and the development of the individual, and which contribute to the feeling of belonging to the human race. Common goods include natural resources, the cultural and historic heritage, social protection, social cohesion, democratic institutions and the sharing of knowledge.

Proximity is a crucial factor. Within regions, towns, neighbourhoods, local institutions, public services, enterprises and the work place it is possible to bring together all the stakeholders required to share social responsibilities. Proximity also encourages the setting up of partnerships and networks, strengthening reciprocity and the stakeholders' confidence in joint action.

7: Principle of non-regression
In order to eliminate poverty, social exclusion and unjustified discrimination, and to secure long-term social cohesion, the preservation of Europe's social and democratic achievements must be guaranteed. Strengthening these achievements is one of the objectives of public policies and of the action of individuals and public and private institutions. No-one may be prevented from exercising their social, civil and political rights or jeopardise their own life and human dignity and everyone should be supported in case of distress.

8: Principle of recognition

The sharing of social responsibilities presupposes the recognition, representation and capacity to influence of everyone, in accordance with his or her needs, contributions and the consequences suffered by him or her.

The views of the weaker stakeholders must be able to be heard, heeded and able to influence decisions and results. This means avoiding situations where the stronger stakeholders, in possession of more information and organisational power relinquish their specific responsibilities, impose priorities based on their interests alone and fail to acknowledge and compensate for the harm to which they may give rise.

Everyone must be able to contribute, individually and collectively, to the well-being of all, future generations included. If some people are incapable of accepting social responsibilities because of circumstances beyond their control, it falls to all parties to rectify the situation.

9: The role of the stakeholders

Sharing social responsibilities in an equitable way requires a reassessment of the allocation of roles and powers among all stakeholders, private and public, and their rights and obligations.

A reassignment of roles, specifying the arrangements for the participation of the various stakeholders in well-being for all and the enjoyment of common goods must take account of the following:

a. the relative urgency of the different expectations expressed by the various stakeholders, acknowledging the priority of those which satisfy fundamental needs and corresponding rights;

b. the possibility of causing harm to others or the risk of having to suffer such harm;

c. the material or non-material contributions of all stakeholders and their corresponding merits.

10: States and governmental authorities
State and governmental authorities are encouraged to promote the sharing of social responsibilities by adopting appropriate legal rules.

To this end, they are required to

a. encourage and legitimise forums for negotiation and discussion between the many stakeholders;

b. motivate stakeholders to comply with the principles relating to the sharing of social responsibilities and the implementation of decisions;

c. make interaction with stakeholders a key opportunity for learning, so that representative democracy and deliberative democracy become mutually reinforcing;

d. communicate information so as to explain the thinking behind public policies enabling a sharing of social responsibilities, and to encourage action to that end;

e. where convincing data are available, promote and publicise the positive results of innovation in the field of social, environmental and intergenerational justice

f. set up institutions specialising in mediation and conflict resolution, facilitating the exercise of shared social responsibility;

g. reassess the role of public servants as mediators between different stakeholders who may have different interests, bearing in mind the constitutional principles and democratic procedures in force;

h. encourage multi-lateral and cross-border activities, including the networking of territories committed to implementing the Council of Europe's Action Plan for Social Cohesion;

i. exchange, develop and codify positive results, in the context of the Council of Europe and with other international organisations.

11: Municipal and local and regional authorities

Local and regional authorities, and especially, city, neighbourhood and village authorities, are encouraged to promote the sharing of social responsibilities. To this end, they are required to:

a. strengthen consistency between the objectives of social, environmental and intergenerational justice, decided by common accord, and individual and institutional choices;

b. introduce mechanisms of participatory and deliberative governance, making possible the sharing of social responsibilities;

c. conclude agreements with other administrative tiers facilitating the establishment of local participatory structures;

d. foster the involvement of residents in projects of general interest, through the preservation and enhancement of common goods, the landscape, the cultural heritage and all local resources contributing to the strengthening of capital, motivations and shared confidence, while including the diversity resulting from immigration;

e. frame local policies which acknowledge and take into account the contribution made by everyone to strengthening social protection and social cohesion, the fair allocation of common goods, the formation of the principles of social, environmental and intergenerational justice and which also ensure that all stakeholders have a negotiation and decision-making power;

12: Companies

Companies are encouraged to adapt their forms of governance to incorporate the general principles of shared social responsibility, so as to:

a. rethink their aims and operational principles in a context of social, environmental and intergenerational justice, bearing in mind all the costs and impacts of their activity;

b. seek lasting competitive advantages by taking into account societal values and social and ecological needs and adapting production processes, rather than focusing exclusively on reducing labour force costs and the socialisation of environmental harm;

c. comply with national legislation concerning working conditions and make sure they are compatible with international working standards in force;

d. integrate further in decision-making the viewpoints of workers, consumers, those who experience the harmful consequences of production, institutions and the relevant civil society organisations;

e. develop ways of managing relationships and conflicts, both in-house and with the stakeholders in the communities and areas where they are located, in a spirit of dialogue, confidence and mutual respect.

f. make the life cycle of products transparent, from the origin of the raw materials to the management of waste;

g. publish periodic reports on the social and environmental impact of their activities, including those of a financial nature;

13: Financial sector

Banks, credit societies and the financial sector are encouraged to participate in the sharing of social responsibilities. To this end, they are required to:

a. rethink their aims and operating principles in a context of social, environmental and intergenerational justice, ensuring their actions do not weaken public and private institutions, families and individuals as a result of short-term speculative choices;

b. be totally open about their offer of financial products, particularly when such products jeopardise the security and dignity of the weakest;

c. adopt measures to avoid the over-indebtedness of families and individuals.

14: Foundations and stakeholders in the social and solidarity-based economy

Foundations and stakeholders in the social and solidarity-based economy are encouraged to participate in the sharing of social responsibilities, in order to:

a. ensure that economic construction is based on the primacy of human dignity, the protection of common goods and a fair reconciliation between individual and collective needs;

b. develop consumption, saving and investment choices enabling everyone to contribute to social, environmental and intergenerational justice;

c. improve information on the social and environmental impact of their activities;

d. support experimentation and research on shared social responsibility.

15: Media and education

The media, teachers and training staff are encouraged to participate in the sharing of social responsibilities. To this end, they are required to:

a. alert public opinion, pupils and students to the principles and processes of shared social responsibility

b. develop, in an educational context, experiments in the field of sharing social responsibilities

16: Trade unions and organised civil society

Trade unions, associations and non-governmental organisations are encouraged to participate in the sharing of social responsibilities. To this end, they are required to:

a. incorporate the principles of shared social responsibility in their aims and organisational structure;

b. take part in forums for deliberative and participatory democracy which enable shared social responsibility to be exercised;

c. take part in multi-stakeholder, multi-level and multi-sectoral processes;

d. exercise, particularly in the case of trade unions, the right to be informed and consulted and defend the employment rights established by the ILO;

e. subscribe, particularly in the case of NGOs, to the code of good practice for civil participation in the decision-making process, adopted by the Council of Europe's Conference of INGOs on 1 October 2009 [CONF/PLE(2009)Code1].

17: Families and individuals

Families and their members are encouraged to participate in the sharing of social responsibilities. To this end, they are required to:

a. take part in forums for deliberative and participatory democracy which enable shared social responsibility to be exercised;

b. bring their consumption, saving and investment choices into line with the pursuit of social, environmental and intergenerational justice;

c. develop forms of shared social responsibility in their everyday settings and immediate neighbourhood, focusing on harmonious co-existence, bringing up children and young people, sociability, job creation through community links, the enhancement of public areas.

18: Deliberative processes and governance

Deliberative processes are not a substitute for representative democracy; rather they strengthen it and are an essential complement for initiating new policies and bringing citizens, stakeholders and public authorities closer together.

The sharing of social responsibilities calls for such processes making it possible for everyone to put forward their own visions and reformulate their preferences through reasoning and exchanges of views and contribute to the development of shared knowledge, objectives and projects. These processes should make it possible to:

a. bring to the fore and examine in a public, transparent setting the different interests put forward by citizens and stakeholders highlighting their interrelations;

b. reconcile individual preferences and demands with common priorities in the field of social, environmental and intergenerational justice and the well-being of all and reach agreements acceptable to each stakeholder;

c. construct shared visions and knowledge capable of reconciling the aspirations of present and future generations;

d. conclude agreements acknowledged as being fair and which will encourage each stakeholder to honour and implement them in practice;

e. reduce imbalances of power between strong and weak stakeholders on the construction of knowledge and on decision-making;

f. renew the sense of specific responsibilities and broadening the scope of individual and collective choices;

g. reactive the stakeholders' moral and social resources, forms of collective intelligence and democratic skills;

h. highlight the key role of social citizenship in countering the fragmentation of responsibilities of individuals as workers, consumers, savers, investors, etc.;

19: Deliberative process methods

Deliberative processes must be structured in accordance with well-defined methodological principles. Each stakeholder must be able to:

a. interact on an equal footing with other stakeholders, all present and duly represented;

b. have an equal right to information and freedom of expression;

c. hear the viewpoint of others in the context of impartial discussions, seeking a consensus that is as equitable as possible;

d. take part in choosing alternatives and taking decisions;

e. discuss differences of opinion openly and publicise the agreements reached;

f. clarify and take into account the long-term effects and interests of decisions on objectives and means of action, including their impact on the weaker players and on future generations;

g. make commitments and receive guarantees about the implementation of decisions and the respective contributions of the other stakeholders;

h. take part in the construction of criteria to assess decisions and initiatives regarding the well-being of all and in the design and implementation of evaluation procedures.

20: Multi-stakeholder, multi-level and multi-sectoral governance

In order to ensure the effectiveness of co-operative and fair agreements and compliance with the decisions taken, forms of multi-stakeholder, multi-level and multi-sectoral governance should supplement existing institutional structures.

21: Innovation and learning processes

In order to initiate new general policies, particular attention should be paid to multi-stakeholder, multi-level and multi-sectoral initiatives today encouraging institutional and social innovation, especially at local level. Of particular relevance are initiatives seeking to:

a. combat the causes of inequalities, impoverishment and discrimination, making it possible to improve individuals' capacities for equitable participation and ensuring the irreversibility of social rights;

b. improve health and social protection systems and other public services by means of joint decision-making and co-production with users, the companies concerned, service providers and public authorities;

c. create and manage common goods, both material and non-material, as a source of learning skills, mediation and identification of shared interests, including with migrants and minorities;

d. set up companies, social enterprises and co-operatives incorporating into their accounts the interests of the other stakeholders in their forms of socially responsible governance;

e. strengthen resilience and devise sustainable lifestyles in terms of production, consumption, mobility, housing, savings and public and private investment;

f. create social links and networks using the new technologies capable of ensuring a pooling of skills and the formulation of relevant responses to the maintaining of social, environmental and intergenerational justice;

g. promote institutions and professions whose aim is the resolution of conflicts, through the impartial consideration of the interests at stake and by broadening the perspectives of the different stakeholders;

Learning processes should be facilitated at all levels in order to promote and disseminate the most relevant innovations and improve evaluation and governance methods.

22: Final Provisions
Member states are invited to disseminate the Charter and encourage and facilitate implementation of its principles.

23: Voluntary accessions
All interested parties, with the exception of natural persons, may accede to the objectives of this Charter by application to the Secretariat of the European Committee for Social Cohesion (CDCS). The voluntary accession procedure provides for the following, in order:

a. a statement of interest in the general provisions and strategies of the Charter;

b. submission of an account of activities already carried out or in progress relating to the general provisions and strategies of the Charter;

c. formal accession to the Charter.

24: Co-operation
All parties to the Charter are invited to make themselves known to each other, exchange their experiences and identify areas of complementary between their initiatives.

25: Evaluation and revision
Member states and all other parties should at regular intervals evaluate the strategies, action and policies pursued in accordance with this Charter and adapt them in line with changing needs and contexts. Evaluation and revision could be the subject of co-operation at various levels.

2.
Shared Social Responsibility as a Key Concept in Managing the Current *Interregnum*

Mark Davis

Introduction

This paper seeks to contextualise the importance of developing the key concept of shared social responsibilities in response to the current complex of social, environmental, political and economic crises that have come to characterise the first decade of the twenty-first century. I seek to do this by outlining these crises as part of a current period of *interregnum*, a time when many of the old certainties are being eroded and a new age is starting to emerge. From this premise, I aim to put forward practical suggestions that target both the need for systemic and individual behaviour changes that will be required if we are to create a Europe of shared social responsibilities. I will do this through the lens of my own area of expertise, namely research into the social and political consequences of consumerism in a global age, and will introduce the notion of 'responsible consumption' into these debates. I begin, however, by offering an interpretation of the current *interregnum*.

The Current *Interregnum*[1]

'The crisis consists precisely in the fact that the old is dying and the new cannot be born' (Gramsci 1971: 276)

One of the most intriguing statements on the current state of global human societies has been offered by Keith Tester (2009). Informed by the

---
[1] This opening section is adapted from a forthcoming paper: Davis, Mark (2011) 'Bauman's Compass: Navigating the current *interregnum*', *Acta Sociologica*, Issue 2.

above quotation, made in the prison notebooks of Antonio Gramsci, Tester (2009: 25) suggests that the various crises that dominate social life at the dawn of the new century can best be captured by the idea that we are presently living in a period of *interregnum*. The various challenges to established liberal models of representative democracy; the (perhaps not so) sudden uncertainty surrounding the neoliberal principles of global capitalism; and the wider challenge of seeking adaptive solutions to the threat of climate change, would all seem to portend that the twenty-first century is beginning with a dramatic stage of transition away from the social, economic, political, and environmental certainties of the recent past. Bauman (2010a), following on directly from Tester's observation, has ruminated upon the term *interregnum* by noting that it was originally employed to mark that period of acute uncertainty that was felt within society during the constitutional 'gap' created by the transition from one sovereign ruler to the next. Bauman, like Gramsci before him, re-imagines the concept of *interregnum* in such a way that it goes far beyond the routine process of transferring hereditary power and instead helps to capture those seminal moments when an entire social order starts to fragment and to lose its authority, but unnervingly at a time when there is no new social order currently ready to take its place. That is to say: Bauman (2010a) suggests that the very fabric of the 'solid modern' social order that was once founded upon the unity of territory, state and nation, is now falling away and there is no new 'king' or 'queen' made to the measure of the new globalized world of 'liquid modernity'. But precisely which 'old ruler' is it that has just passed?

There has certainly been no shortage of proclamations of that which has ceased to be. Fukuyama (1992) was by no means alone in offering a provocative statement about the 'end of...' something that was previously thought to be an eternal part of human social life. To give a few examples, others have explored the possibilities and consequences surrounding the 'end of geography' (Virilio 2007), the 'end of ideology' (Bell 2000), the 'end of democracy' (Crouch 2004), even the 'end of consumerism' (Soper 2000). If we are to follow the diagnosis offered by Slavoj Žižek (2009), however, we find that the recently deceased 'old ruler' is none other than liberalism itself. In his thought-provoking study, Žižek proposes that the first decade of the twenty-first century has seen both the *political death* of liberalism (represented by the events at the World Trade Centre in 2001) and the *economic death* of liberalism (represented by the Great Global Recession of 2008). These 'two deaths' of liberalism have fostered a culture of acute uncertainty, prompting doubts about the legitimacy, and thus longevity, of extant political and economic structures. This has resulted in challenges to the economic hegemony of neoliberalism, as well as to the presumed 'now and forever' political bedfellows arrangement between liberalism and democracy (Gould 2009; Hardt and Negri 2000; Mouffe 1993, 2000; Schwartzmantel 2005).

Few readers sympathetic to Bauman's account of 'liquid modernity' would doubt that we live in uncertain times (Bauman 2000, 2005, 2006, 2007a). At the end of the first decade of the twenty-first century, individuals appear to be increasingly unsure of how best to go about the business of their everyday lives. At least a part of this difficulty would seem to be that throughout the 1990s, which fostered the era of 'happy globalization' fuelled by economic growth and the hedonistic pursuits of a globalised consumer culture (Bauman 2007b, 2008; Davis 2008; Smart 2009; Ray 2009), men and women have become accustomed to managing uncertainty – whether it is over job-security and the state of the economy at a time of global recession; over our own identities and the shape and strength of our personal relationships; our concerns over the future prospects of ourselves and those of our children; over perceptions of fear and crime in our communities; over our faith in politics and in the integrity of our political leaders and representatives, and so on – increasingly as individuals. And as individuals, set free – although perhaps 'cut adrift' is more accurate – from those modern structures of collective security that were once promised and guaranteed by the 'social state' (Bauman 2007c), in the new century individuals know only how to manage their increasingly privatised concerns as consumers, hoping to find solutions to their problems on the high-street. Having largely ceased to act collectively as citizens who share common troubles, and that were once brought to the fore in a public sphere of civil society that resided in that important space between market and state, the capacity to manage the endemic uncertainty of this current 'liquid modern' *interregnum* is measured in terms of the freedom to choose as a consumer.

The more choice as a consumer (i.e. the more resources one has, both time and money, as the essential ingredients to realising that choice in practice) the more able to negotiate (i.e. to shop around for the solutions to) the daily troubles and frustrations that are a part of everyday life in today's global capitalist societies.

In the current crisis, however, this once simple option of shopping so as to find a greater sense of security and well-being is being fundamentally undermined in a confusing and rather contradictory storm of indignation about the irresponsible acts of ordinary men and women habitually pursuing their customary lives as consumers. That is to say: the consumer model of the life-project – such a seemingly dominant and legitimate pattern to follow, or to aspire to follow, until very recently – has now started increasingly to be targeted for blame as answers are sought to larger social and natural problems. As Žižek (2009: 37) remarks, throughout the current economic crisis – often citing both irresponsible lending and borrowing, as well as adaptation to climate change, as the inspiration for their proclamations – leading public figures from all spheres of life have cited the root cause of shared global problems as being the excessive greed and selfishness of individual consumers, seemingly incapable of exercising the necessary restraint and abstinence in the face of those miscellaneous bright delights of the globalised consumer dreamworlds. By placing the blame squarely upon the already burdened shoulders of individual consumers, Žižek stresses, the extant structures of the global capitalist system itself are seemingly absolved of all genuine responsibility when judged by the subsequent response to the crisis (as are the unseen actions of those 'hidden hands' of the global finance markets whose speculative endeavours most assuredly played their part in the current predicament). And, as if identifying the cause in this way was not provocation enough, the global solution to 'recapitalize' the world's banking system, and the speed with which it was enacted, provides some justification for further irritation. As Žižek (2009: 80) states:

> Saving endangered species, saving the planet from global warming, saving AIDS patients and those dying for lack of funds for expensive treatments, saving the starving children ... all this can wait a little bit.

> The call to 'save the banks!' by contrast, is an unconditional imperative which must be met with immediate action. The panic was so absolute that a transnational and non-partisan unity was immediately established, all grudges between world leaders being momentarily forgotten in order to avert the catastrophe.[2]

Returning to Bauman's analysis, these actions on the part of world leaders amounted to nothing less than the truly remarkable creation of a 'welfare state for the rich' (Bauman 2010: 21), assembled in an instant by immediately employing the full might of global states in order to protect the vested interests of an elite few, whilst the legitimate daily demands of the many were once again simply brushed aside and left for another day. Furthermore, whilst the regular welfare state for the poor continues to be underfunded, left to fall into disrepair, or deliberately dismantled, no such fate awaited the global banking sector, who promptly rewarded this worldwide display of benevolence by refusing to suspend its usual 'bonus culture', even amongst widespread public indignation (Jenkins 2010).

> The moment it was halted at the edge of a precipice by a lavish injection of 'taxpayers' money'. TSB Lloyds bank started lobbying the Treasury to divert part of the rescue package to shareholders' dividends; notwithstanding the official indignation of state spokespersons, it proceeded undisturbed to pay bonuses to those whose intemperate greed had brought disaster on the banks and their clients. (Bauman 2010: 22)

Confronted with the full glare of the apparent injustices and inequalities of the current crisis, one might be forgiven for concluding that there was

---

[2] This is all the more striking when considered in relation to the events at the Climate Change Conference in Copenhagen in December 2009. In spite of the rhetoric before the conference took place, the outcome delivered little other than a 'weak outline of a global agreement' (see: http://www.countercurrents.org/vidal191209.htm) amidst a resurgence of global grudges, particularly between the West and China, with explanations tending to focus upon the lack of time available due to various heavy bureaucratic procedures. Compared to the speed and decisiveness with which the banking sector was saved from catastrophe, it is easy to see why the climate change agenda continues to foster feelings of scepticism around the world.

just cause for an acutely pessimistic analysis of human social life at the end of the first decade of the twenty-first century. There is seemingly sufficient evidence that the era of 'happy globalization', with its promises of consumer prosperity for all, now and forever, was far more contingent than the implicit or explicit advocates of the 'end of history' thesis would have us believe. If Žižek is right, however, and we have witnessed the 'two deaths' of liberalism, then perhaps it is also the case that the current *interregnum* presents as much cause for hope as it does for despair. That is to say: amidst the fallout from the combination of crises across the current social, economic and political spheres, there is also an opportunity afforded by the sudden frailty of the liberal hegemony to rethink global societies in the enduring drive for greater equality, stability and sustainability around the world.

So, having offered this brief interpretation of the current *interregnum*, I will now move on to assess how best we might consider responding to the challenges of the new century and to do this I will start by outlining the notion of 'responsible consumption'. This is because I believe that any adequate response to the current crises demands a fundamental rethink of the role of consumerism in our lives.

Towards Responsible Consumption

Responsible consumption is a new concept that is just starting to emerge within both theoretical and policy-relevant discussions, as well as within wider popular debates about how to 'rethink' consumer behaviour. This has emerged in the light of those challenges that have come to define the first decade of the twenty-first century: the Great Global Recession of 2008 and the increasingly urgent need to seek adaptive solutions to the threat of global climate change. Although it is a little early to offer any final word on the future utility of the concept, it is nevertheless worthy of consideration as a key part of developing shared social responsibilities because it would seem to reveal a growing sense of disillusionment with the 'narrowly individualistic' adaptive behaviours associated with so-called 'green' or 'ethical' consumption.

Simply put, *responsible* consumption represents a belief that there is an urgent need to perceive of our actions, our consumer choices, not just individually, but also socially, co-operatively. The concept is informed by, but at the same time distinct from, debates and issues raised by 'green' or 'ethical' consumption. The difference in meaning is both nuanced and revealing, as it illuminates contemporary concerns over the impact that consuming 'ethically' can have in meeting those challenges identified above. A crucial difference between each these three related concepts is this: 'green', or 'ethical', consumption would appear to some to have become a relatively unthinking, un-reflexive act, co-opted by astute advertising and marketing professionals who have identified – not just a sign of global awareness and resistance amongst informed citizens, but also – something akin to a rather lucrative niche market that can be targeted for profit-generating purposes. That is to say: being an 'ethical' consumer has essentially come to mean simply buying those products and services that have been appropriately labelled as such. Products which fall into the 'ethical' category each provide testimony of their 'ethical' credentials from the various agencies and organisations that have been established for this purpose. And yet, with evermore products and services seen to be experiencing the process of 'greenwashing'[3], the role of marketing and advertising in the sphere of 'ethical' consumption is fast becoming both acknowledged and subject to increasing criticism. As such, those well-meaning individual consumers who are highly-sensitive to the 'ethical' message can often find deciding what to buy highly problematic. In raising the possibility that individual 'ethical' consumption – although a part of the solution – is fast running the risk of becoming little more than simply another profit-driven marketing strategy, the notion of *responsible* consumption implies that there are other ways of making changes to identified patterns of consumption that look beyond the *individual*, beyond the choice of this particular 'ethical' product over that particular 'un-ethical' product at the point of purchase.

---

[3] A search on the internet will offer numerous hits for 'greenwashing', but see especially: http://www.guardian.co.uk/environment/series/greenwash; http://stopgreenwash.org/; http://www.climategreenwash.org/.

Thus, the notion of responsible consumption seeks to move beyond this *individualising* process of making personal 'ethical' consumer choices, in order to explore more social, co-operative and community-based alternatives to the requirement to consume as individuals from private companies. This is, at least in part, motivated by recognition of the fact that consuming 'ethically' is not an option available to everyone[4]. As such, one of the major ideas informing the notion of 'responsible consumption' is both the feasibility and desirability of consuming *less* from the marketplace and becoming far more resilient as communities. This is something that the act of simply choosing one product over another significantly overlooks. From one perspective, consuming *less* could be the most 'responsible' choice and the basis for sharing social responsibility, as it is a genuine option for a far wider socio-economic demographic than the increasingly normative requirement to purchase the often relatively more expensive organic or 'fair trade' goods and services. This is a persuasive point: it is surely problematic for all those who would wish to heed the message of needing to consume 'ethically' if they nevertheless lack the necessary resources to be able to afford to make those choices at the point of purchase. This can be represented neatly as a fundamental tension between 'values' (principles) and 'value' (price), and something that simply consuming *less* – rather than simply consuming *differently* – seeks to resolve.

Responsible consumption is an explicit attempt to break out of what we might call, following Herbert Marcuse (2002 [1964]), the 'one-dimensional' role of the *individual* consumer as a passive user of public goods and private services, and proposes a move towards a new model of 'co-production'[5] – i.e. the collective initiation of projects on the basis of actual material needs of sustenance and quality of life and the

---

[4] There are links here to the discussion of 'capacities' in the section 'Towards Shared Responsibilities' in this article.

[5] For more on the idea of 'co-production', see the contribution by Anna Coote in this issue of *Trends in Social Cohesion*. Also, see the following publication by the *Joseph Rowntree Foundation*, which builds directly upon pioneering research by *The New Economics Foundation*: http://www.jrf.org.uk/publications/co-production-people-outside-paid-employment.

implementation of them jointly with producers. The approach is to develop socially responsible consumer networks in order to create a support group for the 'co-production' of goods and services that will meet specific local needs. A good example of this approach can be found in the rising trend towards 'community-supported agriculture', as explored by Thompson and Coskuner-Balli (2007), as well as the web-based networks established at *Freecycle*[6] and the *Furniture Re-Use Network*[7].

What stands behind each of these initiatives is the idea of 're-skilling', of individuals and community groups becoming much more resilient in the hope that they can rely far less on the rampant, 'irresponsible' consumption of the past and perhaps genuinely begin to move towards a 'post-consumerist' future (Soper 2007) in order that we may make use of all our creativity, capabilities and skills beyond simply our ability to shop. And there is plenty of evidence that this is taking place already, as individuals come together to form groups that are offering creative solutions to our shared problems in the global consumer societies of today. As we have seen from the impact of *Transition Towns* and *ecomotion* in the UK, *Cittaslow* in Italy[8], and countless other examples, there is a rising number of socially responsible consumer networks, where local people come together to harness those existing skills within the community in order to provide goods and services and share responsibility for meeting their specific needs.

In close, then, the notion of responsible consumption seeks to overcome the common process whereby individual consumers buy anonymous products from anonymous producers. By collectively negotiating production at a local level in order to meet local needs, the aim is to reintegrate individuals into communities and foster collective values in order to promote well-being and social cohesion – in essence, seeking an alternative to the individualising processes of private consumption, something that simply purchasing 'ethical' goods does not necessarily

---

[6] www.freecycle.org
[7] www.frn.org.uk
[8] http://www.transitiontowns.org/; http://www.ecomotion.org.uk/; http://www.cittaslow.org.uk/

address. By becoming more reflexive, by rationalising individual acts of consumption through an exploration of the broader implications of individual consumer choices and imaginatively exploring alternative ways in which collectively to meet the needs of individuals and communities, responsible consumption implies that it is possible to begin to re-shape global societies for the greater well-being of all. In this sense, then, responsible consumption is a concept that seeks to capture a variety of existing and emerging practices that seek to overcome the 'one-dimensional' approach that would see market-based solutions as the only viable response to the global challenges we face together. Simply being able to buy 'fair trade' products should not also mean that we cease to ask the important wider question: why isn't all trade fair?

And so, whilst undeniably recognising the importance of continuing to consume 'ethically', responsible consumption seeks to recognise those who would now take the next step and move beyond the *individualising* logic of this approach in order to address the wide social context within which individual behaviour takes place. As such, it points to a potentially much wider and more radical shift in attitudes and behaviour. In order to develop this point further, I will now move on to explore this wider social context through a discussion of the different capacities of individuals to become responsible consumers and thus also to foster a sense of shared social responsibilities.

Towards Shared Social Responsibilities[9]

In one of his conversations with Keith Tester (2001), the sociologist Zygmunt Bauman remarks that in today's societies the dominant perception is that "power is measured by the speed with which responsibilities can be escaped" (cited in Fearn 2006). Given this, it is a

---

[9] This section draws heavily upon the following paper: Middlemiss, L. (2010) 'Reframing Individual Responsibility for Sustainable Consumption: Lessons from Environmental Justice and Ecological Citizenship', *Environmental Values*, 19, 147-167.

matter of the greatest urgency to develop a sense of shared responsibilities in order that we may collectively address the challenges that each of us face at the dawn of the twenty-first century, and for social cohesion and individual well-being to become a baseline reference for our societies. But what do we mean by 'shared social responsibility'? And how might this differ from 'individual responsibility'? This section seeks to explore the notion of shared social responsibility, with specific reference to the different 'capacities'[10] of different social actors to behave and to choose responsibly.

As I outlined above, existing discussions within this context have adhered to a rather individualistic conception of responsibility, with a notable tendency to (over)emphasise *individual* responsibilities in the framing of solutions to environmental problems within the context of adapting (individual consumer) behaviours so that societies can become more sustainable. It is also instructive for us to consider a broader sociological framework within which to understand responsibility, because this is a framework that incorporates both individual and shared social responsibility. Part of the problem here, after all, is the focus upon individual responsibility without an equal awareness of and thus emphasis upon how responsibilities are shared across different social actors, organisations and groups. That is to say: individuals often do not have an accurate appreciation of the very real boundaries to their own responsibility – including a recognition of the limits to what it is and is not possible to achieve as an individual – and so rarely link the responsibility for living more sustainable lives to wider structural players (e.g. business and government) within societies. In short, the individualising approach within narratives on sustainable consumption research and policy-proposals tends to focus too narrowly on "the consumer as the principal lever of change" (Sanne, 2002).

By way of example, consider the well-known model of the "ecological-footprint", which implicitly judges the individual consumer and her/his success or failure in meeting their individual ecological responsibilities,

---

[10] The word 'capacity' here is used to mean the ability of the individual to take on responsibility

without any recognition of the very real structural constraints that often frustrate attempts to live more responsibly. What the carbon footprint model fails to acknowledge, therefore, are the *social* reasons 'why' individuals behave in the ways they do. That is to say: my carbon footprint may be tiny, a source of personal pride, but this may be because I have adequate resources, access to good public transport, a local 'organic' farm shop nearby, my own vegetable plot at a local allotment, and no need to drive or to fly anywhere during the course of my working week. However, my carbon footprint may be vast, a source of personal shame, but this may be because there is simply no adequate public transport where I live, and no local shops left because of the enormous supermarket that just opened nearby; plus I have no outside space to grow my own food and the only job I can find requires a two hour commute in the car every day. What the carbon footprint model overlooks – or worse still, considers irrelevant – is the *social* setting within which individuals make their choices and so act out their daily lives, and so it misses a crucial point about why we behave as we do.

Such tendencies towards an 'individualization' of responsibility are a consequence of the wider neoliberal movement introduced in earnest throughout the 1980s with the intention of reducing the role of the State by shifting the locus of responsibility to the individual, specifically to the individual consumer (Maniates 2002; Middlemiss 2010). Maniates, in particular, highlights how such a strategy frames individual 'laziness' and 'ignorance' as the *cause* of social and environmental problems, whilst marginalising wider structural influences on individual behaviour. In so doing, it is unwilling or unable (unable because unwilling?) to develop more substantive solutions that take account of the shared social basis of responsibility.

As a discipline, sociology offers the most extensive analysis of the role of structure in situating individual behaviour within a wider context of action and constraint. Authors typically stress the importance of social context in giving meaning to their everyday lives. Appreciating that individual behaviour takes place within a wider structural context allows for two additions to our understanding of responsibility: first, that fulfilling responsibility depends upon ability (or 'capacity', which I will discuss in more detail shortly); and second, that individuals clearly have different abilities (or 'capacities') and thus have more or less chance of fulfilling their obligations. In short, what a focus upon responsibilities needs to keep firmly in mind is that some individuals will have more capacity than others to fulfil their responsibilities. This is why we need a concept of shared social responsibilities so as to combat those fragmented and narrow conceptions of responsibility that place the burden solely upon the shoulders of individuals. In this context, it is little wonder that research into consumer behaviour frequently finds that individuals feel 'guilty' about continuing to live so-called unsustainable lives and exhibit a genuine sense of frustration and hopelessness about how best to change their behaviours given the real social-structural constraints upon their everyday lives (Middlemiss 2010)[11].

To illustrate this point further, it is worth taking the issue of sustainable consumption as a specific example. By emphasising the role of the individual consumer as both the creator of, and solution to, climate change, there is a built-in normative claim that the producers of goods and services act to fulfil their responsibility (in following preferences that lead to favourable outcomes) whilst the consumers fail in their responsibility (by taking the 'wrong' choices and behaving in 'irresponsible' ways). This emphasis upon the individual responsibility of consumers is far from inevitable, however, and by exploring both the limits of individual responsibilities and the interactions between individual and societal responsibilities, further insights and strategies start to suggest themselves.

A crucial first step is that the responsibilities of the individual could be *reframed* as those of society, shifting the emphasis from individual agency also to include social structure in explaining the causes of and solutions to the issue of sustainability (Spaargaren, 2003; Southerton *et al.*, 2004). The

---

[11] Structural constraints is here intended to include the various resources available to the individual (economic, cultural, social), the normative pressures on the individual (for instance, the requirements of 'fitting in' with the actions of others), and the material and infrastructural arrangements to which the individual is subject (e.g. the spatial proximity of services that serve to enable choices).

individual's responsibility to live a sustainable lifestyle can be reframed to include the responsibility of society to provide the necessary infrastructures that enable individuals to live sustainable lives. In order to foster a sense of shared social responsibility, therefore, the responsibilities of society could also likewise be *reframed* as the right of an individual. In sum: the individual can be seen to have the right to live a sustainable lifestyle and therefore the right to be provided with the resources and opportunities to do so by a fundamental restructuring of society.

In this context, it is useful to emphasise the following points that are drawn from Middlemiss (2010):

1. Considering sustainable consumption in the context of justice and citizenship leads to a more subtle understanding of responsibility for sustainable living, which does not automatically accrue to the individual, but is rather a *shared* obligation between individual and society.
2. Justice and citizenship perspectives suggest that responsibilities are likely to differ between individuals given people's ability to engage with change and the nature of the social context within which they operate.

The crucial point is clearly this: the notion of shared social responsibilities takes into account the differing capacities of individuals to engage with society in pursuit of a more sustainable and inclusive way of life and thus appreciates fully the social structural context within which individual behaviour takes place. To elaborate, it is instructive once again to consult Middlemiss (2010) who identifies four key capacities that enhance the possibilities of sustainable living, but which also provide the basis for fostering shared social responsibilities:

1. Cultural Capacity
Cultural capacity refers to the norms and values that a person holds and how these affect that individual's ability to take on responsibility. The main point here is that if sustainability is somehow connected to a person's world view, then they are more likely to be enabled to act than if their world view does not relate to sustainability. This is not to say that only a

limited set of world views or cultures are compatible with sustainability, but rather that different connections to sustainability can be made differently by different cultures. Focusing upon norms and values is key in order to foster a sense of shared social responsibilities, as this will provide the 'roots' to new decision-making processes and will also help to integrate citizens into a wider process of interaction and dialogue. This is crucial, as it avoids the notion that preaching 'from above' is sufficient to have the desired impact. The distinction is one between *normative* compliance (voluntary, in relation to an identified and agreed norm) and *coercive* compliance (enforced, often in conflict with agreed norms) with the former being much more effective.

2. Organisational Capacity

Organisational capacity refers to those resources offered by organisations that a given individual has contact with. Having regular contact with organisations that somehow support an ideal of sustainability (be that in work, home, or community life), then they are better enabled to take on responsibility for sustainable practices. Organisational support might be in the form of an overall agreement with broadly defined goals of sustainability, or a regular engagement with sustainable practices in the day to day work of the organisation. As above, the principle is one of fostering shared norms and values in order to create a social context within which responsibilities can be shared.

3. Infrastructural Capacity

Infrastructural capacity is interpreted here in a very broad sense, referring to the provision of products and services to the individual by government, business or the community and how these can be brought into line with a given agenda. One suggestion, from the field of sustainable consumption, would be to establish a universal standard labelling index to identify the impact of infrastructures on environmental and societal resources, in order to move beyond regarding the individual as both the principal cause of and the solution to climate change.

4. Personal Capacity

Personal capacity includes a broadly positive attitude to the society and the environment and an understanding of the problems and challenged faced, coupled with the skills of reflexivity, knowledge, enthusiasm, negotiation, motivation, and curiosity. The personal capacity to act is increased if the above three capacities are all already enhanced, as individuals no longer feel isolated and frustrated by the burden of responsibility being solely upon their shoulders. In seeing other individuals, communities and organisations 'sharing responsibility' in this way, individuals are further encouraged to participate more fully as their particular social context and resources allow.

In the context of shared social responsibility, then, there are two major conclusions to draw from the article by Middlemiss (2010):

1. First, appreciating the *social* context of individual behaviour necessarily implies that some actions are difficult (or impossible) for some people as a result of their own capacities and those of the structural context which they inhabit. The importance of this insight cannot be overstated because it challenges both academics and policy-makers to think about the feasibility of the demands made of individual citizens (in the name of sustainable consumption, or assuming greater levels of responsibility), who – given their social and personal context – are very far from a single homogenous group. It could also help to address those identified feelings of 'guilt' associated with 'unfulfilled responsibility' when individuals are unable to act, in spite of sharing the norms and values that encourage them to do so. Structural constraints have to be addressed if shared social responsibility is to become a meaningful and realistic concept in practise.
2. Second, and as a consequence of the above, an individual's responsibility is not always easy and straightforward to ascribe. As the boundaries of individual responsibility are subject to the above capacities, the precise responsibility of an individual for their actions is likely to be a matter of on-going debate. In sum, individuals will have differing capacities and so ought to have different expectations placed upon them. *Those who have the most advantageous matrix of capacities and who are thus better able to accept greater responsibility for the well-being of all should do so.*

It is crucial therefore that, in the name of shared social responsibilities, individuals are fully aware of precisely how responsibility is being shared amongst a wider set of actors (public, private, government, etc) who will all have differentiated capacities to act and make more of a contribution. In close, by framing responsibility within social context, we can move beyond the discourse of individual responsibility fostered by neoliberalism and instead encourage more collective, socially-cohesive strategies that include both public and private actors. It is essential that shared social responsibilities are established as a baseline reference for our societies if we are to respond adequately to the complex of crises that dominate the twenty-first century and move towards a smart, sustainable and inclusive future in Europe. A key first step in this process, I suggest, is to appreciate a basic sociological point by recognising the wider social context within which individual behaviour takes place.

Beyond the Current *Interregnum*...

Taking account of all of the above, what would a 'better society' beyond the current interregnum actually look like? Having developed this paper with specific reference to consumerism, I am certainly not proposing that the goal is to stop consuming completely. Human societies have always consumed in one form or another and will need to do so in the future. But this should not be taken as an insurmountable obstacle to rethinking both 'how' and 'why' we consume, as well as the 'rate' at which we currently consume[12].

As I see it, the goal is to strike a more responsible balance between our individual role as a consumer and our wider roles as citizens, friends, family members, colleagues and members of communities and that one way of trying to achieve thus is to seek solutions at the social level, rather than the individual level. As noted above, the current neoliberal belief in the free market as the single legitimate solution to our shared global

---

[12] As mentioned above, it should be possible to develop a new culture of consuming less by fostering the notion of responsible consumption.

problems doesn't allows us to achieve this sense of balance, nor the sense of shared social responsibility that the papers in this volume are aiming to promote. Responses to the current *interregnum* that focus too narrowly on shifting the behaviour of individuals run the risk of simply repeating the mistake of those who follow the neoliberal belief in focusing solely upon the individual unit, thus regarding the private actor in the marketplace as both the cause of – and, curiously, also the solution to – all of the problems we currently face. For too long, I propose, society has adhered to this neoliberal position and as a consequence it has been reshaped and remodelled in order to serve the needs of a particular economic framework. It is now time for the economic framework to be reshaped and remodelled in order to serve the needs of society.

With the resurgence of interest in the writings of Maynard Keynes, following the soul-searching in the immediate aftermath of the Great Global Recession, we are reminded that the market economy has done what it set out to achieve. It has created a world of abundance, both in terms of the financial wealth generated and the standard of living that we are able to offer to our citizens. The enduring challenge of our times is how these abundant resources continue to be inequitably distributed within societies around the globe. In the face of such abundance, *scarcity should no longer be a problem for any of the world's global inhabitants.* The fact that scarcity so evidently remains a problem is a condemnation of social arrangements at the systemic level, rather than the fault of individual actors behaving irresponsibly.

Fundamentally, we need to shift from a 'market state' to a 'social state', which will require new ideas and concepts, new forms of political action, support from the business community (who are increasingly sensitive to the 'green agenda'), as well as new laws and regulations to buttress the changes against the inevitable and predictable challenges from the few who benefit from the current system to the detriment of all. One of the most corrosive processes to affect our political structures is the perception (too often supported by evidence) that the current neoliberal system works in the interests of an elite few rather than the many. This perception breeds suspicion, cynicism and disillusionment that undermines our democracies and it is for these reasons that we need the kind of fundamental systemic change that can foster new values and norms amongst individuals.

Of course, this is not a simple proposal. How might we begin to make changes at the systemic level? In order to draw together all of the issues raised in this article and offer a conclusion, I would like to offer two proposals that I believe should inform the development of shared social responsibilities and help us all to move beyond the current interregnum.

To begin, as sociologists are well-aware, for genuine social change to take place there are typically four key criteria that need to be met:

1. A strong sense of grievance that something is going badly wrong with the current system
2. A hopeful vision of something better that mixes desirability with feasibility
3. The creation of a group of people strong enough to make that change happen
4. Finally, an event or significantly visible turning point that provides the catalyst for a fundamental rethink about the way society is organised and what purposes it serves

I propose that all four of these conditions are now either in place, or beginning to emerge in increasingly visible ways. There are a host of academics, policy-makers and progressive organisations throughout Europe and beyond who are each trying to shape a vision of a better society for all. Drawing upon some of this work, as well as my own research on the social and political consequences of consumerism, these are my concrete proposals for how we can begin to create a better society that secures the well-being of all:

1. *Greater regulation and / or a 'social tax' on advertising?*
   There are important precedents here. Regulation in Sweden has banned advertisements targeting young people for decades (Plogell and Sundstram 2004). There is a wealth of literature on the damaging

effects of advertising on our young people, not least that they do not have the space in which to become citizens before they adopt the role of consumer (e.g. Barber 2008; Mayo and Nairn 2009; Schor 2006). From infancy, children are a target market for advertisers and are quickly socialised into the role of *homo eligens* – a 'choosing' being – so that the chances of becoming a citizen first and then a consumer second are drastically reduced.

There are also examples of policies from further afield. Sao Paulo in Brazil – one of the most significant 'emerging world economies' – has banned all billboards in public spaces, returning civic life to the people and limiting the impact of commercial interests in our lives (Rohter 2006). Nowhere is this required more urgently than in the UK, I think, where public space in major cities is almost entirely dominated by the visual pollution of advertising, either through traditional or new interactive billboards, or large digital screens.

A more radical suggestion – in line with the Tobin Tax[13], or what has recently been re-labelled the 'robin hood tax'[14] as the idea receives evermore celebrity endorsement –is the feasibility and desirability of introducing a 'social tax' on advertising revenue? After all, we are bombarded with up to 3500 sales shots each day, equivalent to one every 15 seconds of our waking lives. In 2004, companies worldwide spent more than £200 billion on advertising. In the past decade, the number of British TV advertising spots has increased from 3000 to 8000 and the number of available channels multiplied from four to 123 with the introduction of cable/satellite broadcasting (World Advertising Research Centre 2004). A 'social tax' on advertising would help to address both the horizontality and verticality of shared social responsibilities, as those who benefit most directly from advertising are also required to make a contribution to the collective good, through

---

[13] For a brief history of the Tobin Tax, see
http://www.telegraph.co.uk/finance/financetopics/financialcrisis/6521360/The-Tobin-Tax-a-brief-history.html.
For further discussion, see: http://news.bbc.co.uk/1/hi/8264774.stm.

[14] http://robinhoodtax.org.uk

increasing the level of revenue that they generate for social (rather than private, commercial) ends. Again, the burden of shared social responsibilities ought not to fall upon the shoulders of individual consumers alone (in choosing to buy this or that product), but must be shared – and, crucially, must be *seen* to be shared – amongst all members of our society.

Finally, why do we not harness the incredible imagination of creative industries such as marketing and advertising for socially-useful (rather than privately commercial) ends? The 'social advertising' movement in the UK is emerging, as it is in Italy through organizations like *Fondazione Pubblicità Progresso*[15], and so there are existing trends in this direction that could be further developed.

2. ***Address the 'work-time' balance and introduce 'co-production' models***
In the UK, we work more hours than any other nation in the European Union – an average of 42 hours per week (*The Independent*, 23 Feb 2006). A clinical study found that people who work 41 hours or more a week are significantly more likely to have high blood pressure than those who work for less (Yang 2006). A survey presented to the European Parliament in Brussels in 2007 predicted that the stress of over-scheduled lives means that 60% of middle-aged adults will suffer from high-blood pressure by 2027. (Kanavos, P. et al, 2007). One of the principal drivers of this trend is the emergence of a culture of *over-working* whereby status is increasingly attached to being 'over-worked' as a sign of success. A study by the Institute for Social and Economic Research in the UK concludes that: 'Busyness, and not leisure, is now the badge of honour' (Gershuny 2005).

The need to address the 'work-time' balance in order to enhance the capacity of citizens to share social responsibilities is supported by a wealth of argument about the need to reconsider the nature and primacy of economic 'growth' as a measure of prosperity and progress. Smart, sustainable and inclusive societies that promote the well-being

---
[15] http://www.pubblicitaprogresso.it/

of all will need to consider very carefully how the existing commitment to growth at all costs facilitates or frustrates the development of shared social responsibilities. Our habitual insistence that GDP is the only measure of well-being that matters has been undermined frequently in recent times and no longer provides a meaningful indicator of the well-being of our societies (Jackson 2009; McKibben 2007). Indeed, the need to move 'beyond GDP' has become a primary consideration at the European level in recent years[16].

As such, 'progress' towards a better society ought to be measured as achieving a levelling out of the discrepancies between rich and poor, leading to a reduction in inequalities and injustices. This is an increasingly urgent situation. To give just one example, a recent report has demonstrated that in the last decades the UK has become an increasingly divided nation where the richest 10% of the population are now more than 100 times as wealthy as the poorest 10% of society[17]. By any reasonable measure, this is not progress.

---

[16] http://www.beyond-gdp.eu/
[17] The report by the *National Equality Panel*, entitled 'An Anatomy of Economic Inequality in the UK', scrutinises the degree to which the country has become more unequal over the past 30 years. Researchers analyzed inequality according to a number of measures; one indicates that by 2007-8 Britain had reached the highest level of income inequality since soon after the Second World War. The new findings show that the household wealth of the top 10% of the population stands at £853,000 and more – over 100 times higher than the wealth of the poorest 10%, which is £8,800 or below (a sum including cars and other possessions). When the highest-paid workers, such as bankers and chief executives, are put into the equation, the division in wealth is even more stark, with individuals in the top 1% of the population each possessing total household wealth of £2.6m or more.
Although critical of the New Labour government, the paper also indicates that considerable responsibility lies with the Conservatives, who presided over the dramatic divisions of the 1980s and early 1990s, and thus is likely to have made uncomfortable reading for the current coalition government in the UK.
Commissioned by Harriet Harman, then Minister for Women and Equality, the *National Equality Panel* has been working on the 460-page document for 16 months, led by Prof John Hills, of the London School of Economics. The report follows research published by *Save the Children* which revealed that 13% of the UK's children were now living in severe poverty, and that efforts to reduce child poverty had been stalling even before the recession began in 2008.
For further details, see:
http://www.equalities.gov.uk/national_equality_panel/publications.aspx.
For a wider discussion of the report, see:
http://www.guardian.co.uk/society/2010/jan/27/unequal-britain-report.

As with the proposal for a 'social tax' advertising, there are existing trends in this direction that could be further developed. The important work of the *New Economic Foundation*[18] in the UK has opened up the debate on the urgent need to rethink our current use of resources – wealth, time, knowledge and skills – and has proposed alternative models of work and employment that take account of the need to develop the core economy and enhance co-production.

To conclude, I suggest that it is only through fostering *shared social responsibilities* that those with the greatest 'capacity' to act can demonstrate their commitment to *sharing* (rather than simply *transferring*) responsibility. Only by developing shared social responsibilities will we be in a position to crown a new 'ruler' that is made to the measure of the current complex of social, environmental, political and economic crises that have come to characterise the first decade of the twenty-first century and to move with hope beyond current *interregnum*.

---

[18] In particular, see the report: Coote, A., Simms, A. and Franklin, J. (2010) *21 Hours: Why a shorter working week can help us all to flourish in the 21st century*. New Economics Foundation. Available at:
http://www.neweconomics.org/publications/21-hours.

References

Barber, B.R. (2008) *Consumed: How Markets Corrupt Children, Infantilize Adults and Swallow Citizens Whole.* W.W. Norton & Co.

Bauman, Z. (2010) *Living on Borrowed Time: Conversations with Citali Rovirosa-Madrazo.* Polity Press.

Bauman, Z. (2010a) 'The Triple Challenge', in M. Davis and K. Tester (eds) *Bauman's Challenge: Sociological Issues for the Twenty-First Century.* Palgrave Macmillan.

Bauman, Z. (2007a) *Liquid Times: Living in an Age of Uncertainty.* Polity Press.

Bauman, Z. (2007b) Consuming Life. Polity Press.

Bauman, Z. (2007c) 'Has the future a Left?', *Soundings*, 35, available at: http://www.lwbooks.co.uk/journals/articles/bauman07.html

Bauman, Z. (2006) *Liquid Fear.* Polity Press.

Bauman, Z. (2005) *Liquid Life.* Polity Press.

Bauman, Z. (2000) *Liquid Modernity.* Polity Press.

Bauman, Z. and Tester, K. (2001) *Conversations with Zygmunt Bauman.* Polity Press.

Bell, D. (2000) *The End of Ideology: On the Exhaustion of Political Ideas in the Fifties,* second edition. Harvard University Press. [First published in 1960]

Crouch, C. (2004) *Post-democracy.* Polity Press.

Davis, M. And Tester, K. (eds) (2010) *Bauman's Challenge: Sociological Issues for the Twenty-First Century.* Palgrave Macmillan.

Fearn, N. (2006), 'NS Profile: Zygmunt Bauman',*New Statesman*, January 16.

Fukuyama, F. (1992) *The End of History and the Last Man*. Penguin Books.

Gershuny, J. (2005) 'Busyness as the badge of honour for the new super-ordinate working class', *Social Research*, 72, 2: 287-314.

Gould, B. (2009) 'Constructing a Left Politics', *Soundings*, 42: 129-139, available at: http://www.bryangould.net/id79.html

Gramsci, A. (1971) *Selections from the Prison Notebooks*, ed. and trans. Q. Hoare and G. N.

Smith. Lawrence and Wishart.

Hardt, M. And Negri, A. (2000) *Empire*. Harvard University Press.

Jackson, T. (2009) *Prosperity without Growth: Economics for a Finite Planet*. Earthscan Ltd.

Jacoby, R. (1999) *The End of Utopia*. Basic Books

Jenkins, S. (2010) 'The most brazen disdain for democracy in modern times', *The Guardian*, January 13, available at: http://www.guardian.co.uk/commentisfree/2010/jan/12/disdain-democracy-bankers-bonuses-theft

Kanavos, P. Ostergren J., and Weber M.A. (2007) *High blood pressure and health policy: where we are and where we need to go next.* Ruder Finn Inc

Maniates, M. (2002) 'Individualization: plant a tree, buy a bike, save the world?', in T. Princen, M. Maniates, & K. Konca (eds) *Confronting Consumption*. MIT Press, pp. 43-66.

Marcuse, H. (2002 [1964]) *One-Dimensional Man*. Routledge Classics.

Mayo, E. and Nairn, A. (2009) *Consumer Kids: How Big Business is Grooming Our Children for Profit.* Constable.

McKibben, B. (2007) *Deep Economy: Economics as if the World Mattered.* Oneworld Publications.

Middlemiss, L. (2010) 'Reframing Individual Responsibility for Sustainable Consumption: Lessons from Environmental Justice and Ecological Citizenship', *Environmental Values*, 19, 147-167

Mouffe, C. (1993) *The Return of the Political.* Verso.

Mouffe, C. (2000) *The Democratic Paradox.* Verso.

Plogell, M. And Sundstram, J. (2004) 'Advertising to Children in Sweden', *Young Consumers: Insights and Ideas for Responsible Marketers*, 5, 2: 65-68.

Ray, L. (2009) 'After 1989: Globalization, Normalization, and Utopia', in P. Hayden and C. El-Ojeili (eds) *Globalization and Utopia: Critical Essays*, pp. 101-116.

Rohter, L. (2006) 'Billboard ban in São Paulo angers advertisers', *New York Times*, 12 December.

Available at: http://www.nytimes.com/2006/12/12/world/americas/12iht-brazil.html

Sanne, C. (2002) 'Willing consumers - or locked-in? Policies for a sustainable consumption', *Ecological Economics*, 42: 273-287.

Schor, J.B. (2006) *Born to Buy: The Commercialised Child and the New Consumer Culture.* Simon & Schuster Ltd.

Schwarzmantel, J. J. (2005) 'Challenging neoliberal hegemony', *Contemporary Politics*, 11, 2/3: 85-98.

Smart, B. (2009) 'Made in America: The Unsustainable All-Consuming Global Free-Market "Utopia"', in P. Hayden and C. El-Ojeili (eds), pp. 117-136.

Soper, K. (2007) 'The other pleasures of post-consumerism', *Soundings*, 35, March: 31-40.

Soper, K. (2000) 'Other Pleasures: The Attractions of Post-consumerism', *Socialist Register*, 36.

Southerton, D., Warde, A. & Hand, M. (2004) 'The limited autonomy of the consumer: implications for sustainable consumption', in D. Southerton, H. Chappells & B. Van Vliet (eds) *Sustainable Consumption: the Implications of Changing Infrastructures of Provision*. Edward Elgar, pp. 32-48.

Spaargaren, G. (2003) 'Sustainable Consumption: A Theoretical and Environmental Policy Perspective', *Society & Natural Resources*, 16, 8: 687 – 701

Tester, K. (2009) 'Pleasure, Reality, the Novel and Pathology', *Journal of Anthropological Psychology*, 21: 23–26.

Thompson, C.J. and Coskuner–Balli, G. (2007) 'Enchanting Ethical Consumerism: The case of Community Supported Agriculture', *Journal of Consumer Culture*, November, 7, 3: 275–303.

Virilio, P. (2007) *The Original Accident*. Polity Press.

Yang, H. (2006) 'Work hours and self-reported hypertension amongst working people in California', *Hypertension*, 48, 4: 744-750.

Žižek, S. (2009) *First as Tragedy, then as Farce*. Verso.

3.
Sharing Social Responsibility in Shaping the Future: A Trade Union Perspective

David Begg

Fear stalks the land. It is not palpable in the sense that not everybody is equally affected but it is noticeable all the same in a myriad of different ways.

It is a fear which arises from the consequences of the economic crisis which hit us with such speed and intensity in 2008 and from the austerity applied to respond to it.

For most people fear manifests itself in the loss of personal economic security. People are afraid of losing their jobs, afraid of losing their homes, afraid they won't have a pension when they retire. Old people worry about relatively small things like losing their bus pass; and big things like hospital care and not being able to get a place in a retirement home if they need it. Young people worry about not being able to go to third level education or about not having any prospect of employment even if they do acquire a good education.

These fears are not in any sense irrational. There is plenty if anecdotal evidence to give them credence and there are individuals in all socio–economic categories–workers, professionals, business people, pensioners and students – who are hurting very badly and who need help. This was epitomised in the case of a former public servant identified as MP MacDomhnaill, who wrote to the *Irish Times* suggesting that he could not pay his mortgage and feed his family at the same time.

Nor does it looks as if these conditions will improve any time soon.

It has been well telegraphed that the spending review to be concluded in the coming weeks will result in somewhere between €3.6 billion and €4 billion being taken out of the economy in 2012. In fact a further €9bn overall is to be taken out over the next four years.

This will compound the deflationary impact of the €20.6 billion that has been cut in three budgets since 2008 producing a cumulative reduction in GDP of 20 per cent. It is difficult to see how austerity of this magnitude will not seriously debilitate public services because this is cutting into muscle. To compound the problem demographic change means that the demand on public services will expand rather than contract over the next few years. An additional 280,000 people will reach the age of 65 in the next 5 to 10 years with the attendant problem that chronic illness will increase by 40 per cent by 2020, for example (VHI,2011). It is already evident that claims on the social welfare budget – most notably in relation to unemployment and children returning to school – are ahead of expectations.

This level of retrenchment is also profoundly mistaken in economic terms. Domestic demand has fallen by 25 per cent since 2008. When car sales are excluded retail sales in May were 5.2 per cent below the same month in 2010, the thirty ninth consecutive month that they have fallen. This trend continued in July when the volume of retail sales fell by half a percentage point over June. Car sales will no longer be a counterbalance with the end of the scrappage scheme. These problems of the retail sector are epitomised in the receivership of the Superquinn company recently. Superquinn is a very long established player with an annual turnover in excess of €400 million and a 7 per cent share of the market.

It is true that exports are performing well at the moment but the growth rate is likely to moderate in 2012. Nevertheless, there will be a balance of payments surplus in 2011. It is also true that the cost of borrowing has improved with bond yields down to 9 per cent on 26 August, but does not make much practical difference immediately for citizens. In an analysis of financial crises over 800 years published last year, Rogoff and Reinhart (2010) conclude that it is not possible for a country to recover through exports alone. Significant employment gains depend on the domestic economy. And so unemployment will remain at over 14 per cent for the foreseeable future. Many people will fall into long term unemployment – half of those on the live register already are – becoming detached from the labour market. The price of austerity is potentially a lost generation.

In any event austerity is not working. In the second quarter of this year GNP was down 4.3 per cent on the previous quarter. There is no concrete evidence of meaningful growth in the economy and without growth to do some of the heavy lifting of adjustment it is not possible to generate the level of primary surplus necessary to allow for debt repayment. Only those addicted to the oxymoronic notion of expansionary fiscal contraction believe that we will return to growth any time soon. It is not working here and it is not working in the UK where similar austerity policies are being implemented.

It is entirely understandable that people want to put the best possible complexion on Ireland's situation. Indeed confidence is itself a factor influencing peoples' spending patterns. But I think we still have to point to the consequences of flawed policy decisions and try to change them. Nevertheless, leaving room for different economic analyses, there are things we can do collectively to get to a better place.

The theme of this conference is 'sharing social responsibility in shaping the future'. It could perhaps be shortened to just one word – solidarity! It is understandable, but nevertheless regrettable, that the last three years have been one great act of constant recrimination. At this point everybody has made up their minds about who is responsible. It has almost been like a grieving process, with different stages of grief. But now we have to try to move on.

Is it possible to embrace the concept of solidarity? What might it mean in practice and how do we go about it? But we also need to be realistic because there are now and always will be conflicting interests in society. All history proves that efforts to build utopia nearly always end in totalitarianism of one kind or another.

Nevertheless, sharing social responsibility, or solidarity as I prefer, offers the opportunity to start imaging the future in more promising terms. The best definition of solidarity that I have encountered came from the late Pope John Paul 11:

"Solidarity ..... is a firm and persevering determination to commit oneself to the common good, to the good of all and of each individual, because we are all really responsible for all"

(Pope John Paul 11, 1987)

We find ourselves in a place today where our future is very much bound up with the future of Europe. The European Union is first and foremost a political project. It is really a melding of the Christian democrat and social democrat traditions to produce the idea of Europe as a way of life. It was born out of a desire to find an accommodation between the extremes of free market capitalism and communism. It is therefore about values, values which are, for example, distinctly different from those of the United States.

The historian, Tony Judt, who died last year, in his history of Europe since 1945 wrote extensively about these differences, noting that mainly free-market critics of Europe's welfare States thought the core problem facing Europe was economic rigidity. There were too many laws protecting wages and jobs, or else guaranteeing such elevated unemployment and pension payments that people lacked all incentive to work in the first case. It is a refrain which has become very familiar to our own ears over the last couple of years. But as Judt pointed out, the fact that labour markets were regulated and inflexible by American standards did not mean that Europe's economies were inefficient or unproductive. In support of this he cited productivity levels per hour worked in 2003. The economies of Switzerland, Denmark, Austria and Italy were all comparable to the US. By the same criterion Ireland, Belgium, Norway, The Netherlands and France all outproduced the US (Judt, 2005:792)

Moreover, the quality of life in Europe is better, mainly through the provision of a wider range and quality of socials services. Europeans were better educated through secondary school than Americans; they lived safer and longer lives, enjoyed better health (despite spending for less) and had many fewer people in poverty. This then, was the 'European Social Model'. It was expensive but for most Europeans its promise of job security, progressive tax rates and large social transfer payments presented an implicit contract between Government and citizens, as well as between one citizen and another. According to the annual Eurobarometer polls an overwhelming majority of Europeans took the view that poverty was caused by social circumstances and not individual inadequacy. They also showed a willingness to pay higher taxes if these were directed to alleviating poverty. According to Judt:

> Such sentiments were predictably widespread in Scandinavia. But they were almost as prevalent in Britain, or in Italy or Spain. There was a broad international cross-class consensus about the duty of the State to shield citizens from the hazards of misfortune or the market: neither the firm nor the State should treat employees as dispensable units of production. Social responsibility and economic advantage should not be mutually exclusive – 'growth' was laudable, but not at all costs.
>
> (Judt, 2005: 793)

It is important to emphasise that this 'European Social Model' of which Judt speaks is a multifaceted creature.

The seminal work on social welfare systems in Europe is that of Gosta Esping Andersen (1990). He classifies countries into four separate welfare regimes viz: A Social Democratic Nordic Model, A Liberal Model associated with the UK and Ireland, a Continental Model derived from Christian Democracy and finally a Mediterranean Model. What they have in common is not a discrete set of services or economic practices, or a particular level of State involvement. To quote Judt again:

> "It was, rather, a sense – sometimes spelled out in documents and laws, sometimes not – of the balance of social rights, civil solidarity and

collective responsibility that was appropriate and possible for the modern State". (ibid).

A few weeks ago I was speaking to a retired senior civil servant who was very committed all his life to the concept of European integration. He expressed his disappointment with the current state of affairs observing that it would be very difficult to advocate in the future for EU initiatives. I must say that I share his disenchantment. It is difficult to disagree with Helmut Kohl's assertion that the current political leadership seems to have lost sight of the bigger picture – the political vision behind integration. I have had a number of engagements with the 'Trokia' and I can come to no other conclusion but that the representatives of the EU and the ECB are of a very doctrinaire free market persuasion. Nor is there much evidence of the cross-class consensus building in the 'Euro Plus' pact for competitiveness.

Leaving our own country out of it altogether, there is a chilling absence of solidarity in the way Greece is presented as a feckless nation of people who are in the single currency for access to cheap money but not in the single market. It is true that Greece has form – fiddling the books and being locked out of international money markets for 53 years – but that was known in large measure before they were admitted to the EMU. Greece has had a very difficult recent history. Tony Kinsella, who sometimes writes a column for *The Irish Times* described it thus:

> "Greece's civil war, the toxic fusion of the legacy of that war with the Cold War and Greek history, and the country's physical location have all acted to hinder the social, political and economic development of the third Hellenic Republic".

(Kinsella, undated: 1)[19]

---

[19] I am indebted to Brendan Halligan for making this unpublished paper available to me.

Finland's attempts to go even further than the terms of the bailout package in forcing unilateral coercive terms for its support of Greece are a case of solidarity with an iron fist (Spiegal, 2011).

One example of a European country where there has been a practical manifestation of social responsibility is France. The willingness of prominent rich citizens to publically state their willingness to take a disproportionate share of the burden of fiscal correction has allowed the Government to apply an 'exceptional contribution' to higher income earners (*Guardian* Editorial Friday 26 August, 2011). I do not expect to see similar developments here.

From a distance it is hard to figure out what is really going on in Europe. One gets the very strong impression that policy is being made via intense intergovernmentalism with the Commission constantly running to catch up. Perhaps Angela Merkel will bow to the inevitability of Euro Bonds as an end game. The price will be twofold: a 'German Europe' rather than a 'European Germany' and deeper European integration.

Deeper European integration presents perhaps the hardest decision for Ireland. The recent visits of Queen Elizabeth and President Obama were in a way a manifestation of a foreign policy that sees Ireland as a multi-interface peripheral country (Ruane, 2010). We are in Europe but not necessarily of it. We balance our Eurozone involvement with equally important economic, and indeed cultural, relationships with Britain and the US. At the moment we have the same relationship to Europe as a hen has to the full Irish breakfast – we are involved! Shortly we may become more like the pig, fully committed! We will have to buy in to a European social model rather than an American one. Whether by that time liberal free market ideologues will have eviscerated the model remains to be seen. In any event deeper integration will foreclose the long running and unresolved Boston V Berlin debate.

In doing so it may open another. What kind of country will Ireland be in a more deeply integrated Eurozone? It is a sobering thought that three times in the last sixty years Ireland has looked into the abyss of economic catastrophe. In the mid 1950s we were rescued by the designs of the first programme for economic expansion (1958) and the adoption of export orientated industrialisation. In the mid 1980s we avoided the clutches of the IMF by embracing Social Partnership and by 1994 the economy was on the road to recovery. But before this recovery many people began to question whether Ireland was a viable political entity at all (MacSharry and White, 2000). Such thoughts were quickly discarded as the country began the most sustained period of economic expansion in its history.

Now that we are in difficulty again these troubling questions return. They will be less easily discarded on this occasion.

The doubts of an earlier era did cause some deeper reflection for a time. In 1991 The National Economic and Social Council asked a Norwegian academic, Prof. Lars Mjoset, to conduct a comparative study of Ireland and a number of small open Northern European economies to find out why we were doing so badly and they were doing so well. By the time his report (Mjoset, 1992) was published the Irish economy had begun to take off and so it was more or less left on the shelf.

There is merit in looking again at this question because Ireland has more in common with the small open economics of Northern Europe in some respects than it has with Greece or Portugal. With exports worth about as much as it's GDP, Ireland is an extraordinarily open economy – far more so than Greece or Portugal (The Economist, 2011). In fact it is much more like Finland and Denmark, both of whom happen also to be among the wealthiest countries in the world.

What distinguishes these small open economies is that they long ago decided that the external competitive threat was such that they had to confine domestic quarrels within certain limits (Karzenstein, 1985). Denmark is an exemplar of this approach. From the mid 1980s Danes began to realise that they needed to restructure their economy to deal with globalisation and the demands of European integration. Restructuring the public sector was seen as the key to making the private sector more efficient and competitive in export markets. Neoliberalism informed this process but never dominated it. Welfare and Labour market reform was tried unsuccessful by conservative governments during the 1980s. However, the social democrat led government elected in 1992 did achieve some progress reflected in the much debated 'flexicurity' model. Reform was achieved via the work of tripartite commissions set up to consider different aspects of social and economic policy. This is defined in the academic literature as creating a 'negotiated economy' (Madsen, 2006; Kjaer and Pedersen, 2001).

Although the Danish State has faced many external challenges, its internal legitimacy has never been seriously disputed. The tradition of collaboration has its roots in the 1700s such that State and civil society have well established ways of interacting. Campbell and Hall (2006) point to the fact that, since the mid 1980s, a very wide array of interests is represented in decision making negotiations. In fact since the Second World War Denmark has consciously sought to combine liberal and social democratic values. The effect of this has been to blur the distinctions between public and private institutions and between State, nation and people. Denmark is also a society characterised by a high degree of trust which lends itself to a culture of compromise, consensus and cross-class collaboration. This is important in the context of Dieter Senghaas' (1982) theory of development. Senghaas finds that some peripheral economies remain less developed by virtue of domestic factors whereas others, like Denmark, can achieve core status even against harsh external conditions (see also Georg Sorensen, 2010). Rory O'Donnell (2010) also emphasis the importance of domestic cohesion and notes that in Denmark's case this is facilitated by religious, ethnic and racial homogeneity and by an active role by the State in organising social classes and other groups. He attributes particular importance to the electoral system of proportional representation as a driver of political power sharing.

Denmark joined the European Community at the same time as Britain and Ireland in 1973. It was motivated by a combination of a desire for active intergovernmentalist and economic motivation although only the latter was emphasised by politicians canvassing support for membership. Kelstrup (2006) writes that there was a change towards greater commitment to the broad European project in 1986 as a result of a change of attitude within the social democrats but this was somewhat derailed by the 1992 referendum on Maastricht.

The importance of EU integration should not be underestimated in terms of the structural changes referred to earlier. Around 1990 the evaluation of structural impediments moved in the direction of adaptation of Danish society as a whole to European integration. The political elite formed the view that the public sector had an important role in changing the political economy of Denmark to match the demands of EU integration and the longer term development of the EU. In the words of Michael Boss:

> 'The result was that Danish society developed into an integrated and coordinated political system of negotiations involving multiple private and public actors on national as well as local levels'.
>
> (Boss, 2010: 270)

Denmark was the fourth most competitive country in the world by 2003. At the same time Denmark managed to remain at once one of the wealthiest societies and the most egalitarian. During the 1990s GDP per capita increased from $18,463 to $22,123 making it the third best OECD country in 1998 and in 1997 it had a Gini coefficient of 0.21 which was the lowest in the EU. During the mid to late 1990s poverty rates were reduced to 4 per cent, again well below the EU average of 12 per cent (ibid).

It is indicative of the Danish outlook on affairs that, alone of all the EU countries, it is implementing a fiscal stimulus of its economy to prevent a double dip recession.

My long held belief is that we should try to emulate the Nordic countries, not just for their economic success but for the social sustainability and equality that is integral to their polity. It is a polity rooted in a political economy approach which holds that the economy is embedded in society and not the other way round. In a political sense these are social democratic countries which, even when governed by liberals or conservatives, largely adhere to a social democratic polity.

Ireland is regarded as being in the liberal Anglo-Saxon group of countries although some scholars qualify this by pointing to some counter tendencies such as an interventionist industrial policy and, for a time, the existence of Social Partnership. (O'Riain, 2004: Smith, 2005). My view of the differences between social democrats and liberals is taken from Tony Judt:

> "Social democrats …are something of a hybrid. They share with liberals a commitment to cultural and religious tolerance. But in public policy social democrats believe in the possibility and virtue of collective action for the collective good. Like most liberals, social democrats favour progressive taxation in order to pay for public services and other social goods that individuals cannot provide themselves; but whereas many liberals might see such taxation or public provision as a necessary evil, a social democrat's vision of the good society entails from the outset a greater role for the State and the public sector".

(Judt, 2010: 5).

Social democracy has never taken root in Ireland. Twenty years ago, the ESRI explained this in the context of our history in which every issue since the foundation of the State was conceptualised in terms of independence. Even membership of the EEC was sold as a means of enhancing our independence notwithstanding the loss of sovereignty inherent in that decision. This militated against the emergence of a class based politics similar to other European countries. It explains perhaps why the Labour Party, which will be 100 years old next year, has never managed to lead a Government in this country (Breen et al, 1990).

The continuing uncertainty over the future of the Euro and the state of the global economy must allow the possibility that Marx was at least partially right in his analysis of the inherent contradictions of capitalism. It is hardly possible that the global economy can continue to produce an ever expanding flow of goods and services if the population cannot afford to buy them.

Writing in the *Financial Times* recently Samuel Brittan recalled that a former Chief Economist of the IMF, Raghuram Rajan, has attributed the credit explosion of the boom years partly to wage stagnation which encouraged people to borrow (Brittan, 2011). Wage stagnation is a product of a change in the balance of power between capital and labour that has taken place over the last twenty years. Mainly this is due to the coming on stream of 1.5 billion new workers as China, India and the countries of the former Soviet Union joined the global economy. This more than doubled the world's industrial workforce virtually overnight and diminished the collective bargaining power of trade unions.

Since the early 1990s Governments in the US, the UK, and the Eurozone pursued inflation-targeting policies designed to smooth out cyclical ups and downs. They used low interest rates to stimulate a debt-driven recovery after the dotcom crash in 2001. The flood of cheap goods from China helped to suppress inflation. It was Greenspan's successor, Ben Bernanke who coined the phrase 'The Great Moderation' to describe this period.

It appeared that stability had been achieved by policy alone. It is now clear that this was not the case. Stability was sustained by the deflationary impact of China, the relentless rise of cheap credit and an altered balance of power between labour and capital. Now the cheap credit model has collapsed and with the need for China to rebalance its economic policy from exports to boosting domestic demand it is likely that its deflationary influence may turn out to be transitory.

The way this 'Great Moderation' model worked could be witnessed here during the boom years when people of modest income could, and did, borrow to buy second homes. Capital appreciation on property created a wealth effect detached from real income. That former wealth effect has become the albatross of negative equity for many. They have no obvious way out of the situation. In short they are trapped and no longer able to buy the goods and services available in the market.

Of course this does not apply to everyone. Indeed there is evidence of increasing inequality in society. This will continue unless people are empowered to achieve a fairer share of society's benefits. This would normally be done through collective bargaining but, for reasons already explained, workers influence has been weakened. That is why Congress has consistently advocated for a legal right to collective bargaining.

The High Pay Commission in the UK reported recently that the FTSE 100 Chief Executives are on average paid £4.2 million annually or 145 times the median wage. By contrast the earnings of someone in the middle of the income distribution rose at less than 0.7 per cent a year over the period 1996/7-2007/8. (Wilby, 2011). This stratification of society can be seen here in the increasing numbers of children attending private schools even during the recession.

The interesting thing about these data is that they indicate that in the liberal market economies at least, the very rich are soaring ahead of not just manual workers but the middle class as well. We are talking here of doctors, teachers, solicitors, academics, civil servants and so on. These are the people who internalised the values of individual aspiration. The recently well publicised case of MP MacDomhnaill already referred to is a manifestation of this phenomenon.

How will this evolution of inequality, involving not just those in the lower socio-economic groups but the middle class as well, play out in the long run? History is not encouraging in this regard. Eric Hobsbawm attributes the rise in Fascism in the 1930s to disaffection amongst the middle classes observing that:

> 'Broadly speaking, the appeal of the radical right was the stronger, the greater the threat to the standing, actually or conventionally expected, of a middle-class occupation, as the framework buckled and broke that was supposed to hold their social order in place'.

(Hobsbawm, 1994: 122)

The conditions we now face in Europe are eerily redolent of the 1930s. Social Europe is very much in retreat. There is no figure like Jacques

Delors to articulate a convincing vision of the future. The crisis calls for a solidarity that the current generation of leaders are either unable or unwilling to command from the citizens. To the contrary. In many European countries Nationalist and Eurosceptic parties are gaining ground.

This is the reality. It is not an environment likely to be receptive to the concept of shared social responsibility. There is a serious distributional justice conflict in prospect arising from the growing inequality I have referred to.

This analysis leads me to the conclusion that we have to find a way to reinvent ourselves as a society. All we have really been presented with so far are solutions based on more extreme versions of a social and economic model that has failed us.

Of course this is most fundamentally about values – about eschewing formulaic economics for a political economy approach. It is about whether the economy subsists in society or whether we just succumb to being a pure competition State in which the interests of investors and business will always trump those of citizens.

Taken seriously the concept of sharing social responsibility – or solidarity – is not as nebulous as it sounds. I have tried to show how it is possible and practical to achieve it using the Nordic model epitomised by Denmark. To be blunt I don't think there is any other way for a small open economy to be wealthy, sustainable, and egalitarian and free from fear.

BIBLIOGRAPHY

Böss, Michael (2010) 'Pragmatic Nationals: The Character and Roots of Danish Europragmatism' in Michael Böss (ed) *The Nation State in Transformation: Economic Globalisation, Institutional Mediation and Political Values.* Denmark. Aarhus University Press.

Breen, Richard et al (1990) *Understanding Contemporary Ireland: State, Class and Development in the Republic of Ireland.* Manchester and New York. Manchester University Press.

Brittain, Samuel (2011) 'Against Wall Street's Mistaken Marxist Moment' *The Financial Times.* August 26th, 2011.

Campbell, John L and Hall, John A (2006) 'Introduction: The State of Denmark' in John L Campbell, John A Hall and Ove K Pedersen (eds) *National Identity and Varieties of Capitalism: the Danish Experience.* Canada. McGill – Queens University Press.

'Celtic Cross: Irelands Chances of Recovery' The Economist. May, 28, 2011: P.69.

Esping–Andersen, Gosta (1990) *The Three Worlds of Welfare Capitalism.* Cambridge. Polity Press.

Hobsbawm, Eric (1994) *The Age of Extremes.* London. Abacus.

'Howls of Anguish: Taxing the Rich' *Guardian* Editorial. August 26th 2011. P. 36.

Judt, Tony (2005) Postwar: *A History of Europe since 1945.* London. Vintage

Judt, Tony (2010) *Ill Fares the Land.* London. Penguin

Katzenstein, Peter (1985) *Small States in world Markets*: Industrial Policy in Europe. New York. Corwell University Press.

Kelstrup, Morten (2006) 'Denmark in the Process of European Integration: Dilemmas, Problems and Perspectives' in John L Campbell and Ove K Pedersen (eds) *The Rise of Neo Liberalism and Institutional Analysis.* New Jersey and Woodstock. Princeton University Press

Kinsella, Tony (undated) *'Krisis' and the Need for Strong and Visionary European Leadership".*

Kjaer, Peter and Pedersen, Ove K (2001) 'Translating Liberalisation: Neoliberalism in the Danish Negotiated Economy' in John L Campbell and Ove K Pedersen (eds) *The Rise of Neoliberalism and Institutional Analysis.* Princeton and Woodstock. Princeton University Press.

MacSharry, Ray and White, Padraic (2000) the making of the Celtic tiger: *The Inside Story of Ireland's Boom Economy.* Cork. Mercier Press

Madsen, Per Kongshoj (2006) 'How Can It Possibly Fly? The Paradox of a Dynamic Labour Market in a Scandinavian Welfare State' in John L Campbell, John A Hall and Ove K Pedersen (eds) *National Identity and Varieties of Capitalism.* Canada. McGill – Queen's University Press.

Mjoset, Lars (1992) *The Irish Economy in a Comparative Institutional Perspective*, Dublin. NESC No.93

Nicola Jo – Ann Smith (2006) *"Showcasing Globalisation the Political Economy of the Irish Republic".*

O'Donnell, Rory (2010) 'Negotiated Governance and Hybridity in Small European Countries: Ireland and Denmark' in Michael Böss (ed) *The Nation State in Transformation: Economic Globalisation, Institutional Mediation and Political Values.* Denmark. Aarhus University Press.

O'Riain, Sean (2004) *The Politics of High-Tech Growth: Developmental Network States in the Global Economy.* Cambridge and New York. Cambridge University Press.

Pope John Paul 11 (1987) Solicitude Rei Socialis

Rogoff, Kenneth and Reinhart, Carmen (2009) This time is Different: Eight Centuries of Financial Folly. Princeton. Princeton University Press.

Ruane, Joseph (2010) 'Ireland's Multiple Interface – Periphery Development Model: Achievements and Limits 'in Michael Boss (ed) *The Nation State in Transformation: Economic Globalisation, Institutional Mediation and Political Values.* Denmark. Aarhus University Press.

Senghaas, Dieter (1982) *The European Experience: A Historical Critique of Development Theory.* Leamington Spa and Dover.

Sorensen, Georg (2010) 'Globalisation and Development: Ireland and Denmark in Comparative Perspective' in Michael Böss (ed) *The Nation State in Transformation: Economic Globalisation, Institutional Mediation and Political Values.* Denmark. Aarhus University Press.

Spiegel, Peter (2011) 'Finnish Deal Faces Revision to Save Bail – Out' *The Financial Times.* August 26th 2011. P.6

VHI (2011) Universal Health Insurance. Presentation by VHI to ICTU May 30th, 2011.

Wilby, Paul (2011) 'Anxiety Keeps Super Rich Safe from Middle Class Rage'. *The Guardian.* May 19th, 2011.

4.
Sharing Responsibility in Building the Future: A Business Perspective.

Danny McCoy

The last occasion on which I spoke to the Social Justice Ireland Annual Social Policy Conference was in June 2008. I was asked to address the theme '*Making Choices: Securing Futures – Ireland at a crossroads*'. Three months later Lehman Brothers collapsed and the world changed. Little did we know that were not so much at a crossroads as on the edge of an abyss.

The ensuing three years have shaped the narrative around today's conference. The capitalist system has been under siege. Business has been viewed as a major cause of social, environmental and economic problems. The Council of Europe's draft charter on shared social responsibilities, the text of which appears at the beginning of this publication, urges companies:

> '*to take account, in their strategies, of the interests of all stakeholders, both internal and external, and of the impact of their activity on society at large, going beyond a reductive view of economic efficiency that ignores collective well-being and drawing inspiration from the principles of the socially responsible and solidarity-based economy*'.

While I agree with the thrust of this sentiment, I can't help feeling that it is derived from a paradigm that pits business and society against each other. This is in part because economists have added legitimacy to the idea that to provide societal benefits, companies must temper their economic success. In neoclassical thinking, a requirement for social improvement – such as improved working conditions or hiring people with disabilities – imposes a constraint on the company. According to this theory, adding a constraint to a firm will inevitably raise costs and reduce these profits.

A related concept is the notion of externalities. Externalities arise when firms create social costs that they do not have to bear, such as pollution. Therefore, society must impose taxes, regulations and penalties so that companies 'internalise' these externalities. This belief still influences many EU and government policy decisions.

In fairness, the draft Charter urges companies to 'seek lasting competitive advantages by taking into account societal values and social and ecological needs.' But this is more than outweighed by exhortations to;

> *review their aims ...bearing in mind all the costs and impacts of their activity*

or to integrate the views of;

> *those who experience the harmful consequences of production.*

I believe that we should be moving beyond a policy approach that institutionalises presumed trade-offs between economic efficiency and social progress. We need to move from a consideration of shared responsibilities to the creation of shared value.

I am not talking about shared personal values. Nor is this about a redistribution approach, 'sharing' the value already created by companies. This is about expanding the total pool of economic and social value. I promoted this idea at this conference three years ago. It's not original. Michael Porter and Mark Kramer proposed it as a new way to look at the relationship between business and society that does not treat corporate success and social welfare as a zero-sum game[20]. Successful corporations need a healthy society, while education, healthcare and equal opportunity are essential to a productive workforce.

---

[20] Porter, M.E. and Kramer, M.R., 2006. Strategy & Society: The Link Between Competitive Advantage and Corporate Social Responsibility. Harvard Business Review, December 2006.

At the same time no social programme can rival the business sector when it comes creating the jobs, wealth and innovation that improve living standards. Choosing which social issues to address, they argue:

> ...is not whether a cause is worthy but whether it presents an opportunity to create shared value – that is a meaningful benefit for society that is also valuable to business. Efforts to find shared value in operating practices and in the social dimensions of competitive context have the potential not only to foster economic and social development but to change the way companies and society think about each other.

The concept rests on the premise that economic and social progress must be addressed using value principles. Value is defined as benefits relative to costs, not just benefits alone. Value creation is an idea that has long been recognised in business, where profit is revenues earned from customers minus the costs incurred. However, business have rarely approached social issues from a value perspective, but tended to treat them as peripheral matters.

The experience of the last three years makes this argument even more compelling. It has been suggested that the current crisis provides evidence that our economic model is broken and must be replaced. I disagree. The market continues to guarantee the most efficient allocation of resources. But I would accept that our recent experience highlights the dangers of viewing value creation narrowly. Business cannot afford to optimise short-term financial performance in a bubble while missing the most important customer needs and ignoring the broader influences that determine their long term success.

Governments and NGOs can enable and reinforce shared value or work against it. For example, regulation is necessary for well-functioning markets, something that became abundantly clear during the financial crisis. However, the approach to the way regulations are designed and implemented, determine whether they benefit society or work against it. Regulation that discourages shared value forces compliance with particular practices, rather than focusing on measurable social improvement. It mandates a particular approach to meeting a standard, thereby blocking innovation and driving up business costs.

Appropriate regulations should set clear and measurable social goals, whether they involve energy use, health matters or safety. Where appropriate, they set prices for resources that reflect true cost. They set performance targets but do not prescribe the methods to achieve them. These are left to companies.

They define phase-in periods for meeting standards, which reflect investment or new-product cycle in industry. Phase-in periods give companies time to develop and introduce new products and processes in a way that is consistent with the economics of their business

They put in place universal measurement and performance-reporting systems, with government investing in infrastructure for collecting reliable benchmarking data. This encourages continual improvement. Finally they require efficient and timely reporting of results rather than expensive compliance processes.

There are signs of change. Efforts to minimise pollution were once thought to inevitably increase business costs and to only occur because of taxes and regulation. We now know that major improvements in environmental performance can be often be achieved with better technology that can even reduce business costs through better resource utilisation, process efficiency and quality. Heightened environmental awareness and advances in technology are also stimulating new approaches in areas such as utilisation of water, raw materials and packaging. Logistics systems are being redesigned to reduce shipping distances, streamline handling and improve vehicle routing.

All of these steps create shared value.

It is also important to remember the context within which we are developing policies of shared responsibilities. This is shaped by global issues over which Europe only has partial influence. These include the rise of new economic powers in Asia and Latin America, higher capital and labour mobility around the world, climate change and the increased competition for natural resources.

Another lesson from our economic crisis is the degree to which Celtic Tiger Ireland became so insular on a range of important economic issues. We justified exorbitant asset prices and bloated salaries on a domestic economic mirage. We convinced ourselves that our circumstances were different to other economies which had experienced market bubbles and we built up a whole raft of public expenditures on unsustainable property related revenues. We completely lost sight of how we compared to most normal developed economies.

Ireland is one of the most open and globalised economies in the world. In order for us to rebuild our economy and get people back to work again we must continuously benchmark ourselves against other successful trading nations.

During the good years our public sector pay rates grew to be amongst the highest in the developed world, our idea of benchmarking was to compare public sector salaries to workers in our domestic economy not to similar positions in our trading partners. We grew our public expenditure at unprecedented rates and everything from education and heath to social welfare rates benefited from the bubble economy. We decided we didn't like income taxes too much so through successive budgets we delivered the lowest effective income tax rates in the OECD and took about half of those at work out of the tax net completely. Some of these expenditure programmes represented catch up for years of under-investment but many of the economic policies taken during this period were entirely unsustainable. It is not a very popular fact but the reality is that every section of society benefited from the property fuelled tax revenues but of course some benefited much more than others did.

Ireland's economic future remains very bright and we retain capacity to deliver growth rates of about double that of the EU average. For this to happen, however, economic policy of the future can't be made in either ignorance or defiance of trends in other countries. We need reasonable taxes to fund our public services; our public sector salaries must be comparable to those of our competitor countries; we must accept the necessity of local charges as part of an effective model of local government; our welfare and tax systems must interact in a manner which incentivises people to take up job offers.

The flaws of the Celtic Tiger economic model were evident to many observers who had spent time living and working internationally. They had seen it all before but yet the consensus in Ireland bought into the 'this time is different' theory. In seeking to rebuild our economy we must be much more open to the experiences of other successful economies.

We must also ensure that our response to the crisis remains focused on the need for Ireland to be flexible, innovative and competitive. Our future prosperity will depend on our ability to exploit global opportunities and to react quickly to changing market trends. Our crisis response cannot be isolationist and it would be counterproductive to pursue economic policies which run counter to developments in other developed countries. It would be futile for Ireland to act unilaterally on policy issues which may gain popular traction in a post crisis society. Our economy and society needs radical reform and change but this must be done in a manner which makes us more successful internationally and allows us to remain attractive for mobile international investment.

Society's needs are huge – health, improved nutrition, help for ageing, greater financial security, less environmental damage. Arguably they are the greatest unmet needs in the global economy. In advanced economies in particular, demand for products and services that meet social needs are rapidly growing. For example, food companies that traditionally concentrated on taste and quantity to drive more consumption are refocusing on the fundamental need for better nutrition. Some ICT companies are devising ways to help utilities to harness digital intelligence in order economise on power usage. Others are addressing the physical, cognitive and social consequences of ageing by using new technologies to help older people maintain their independence and to age in their own homes.

In these and many other ways, whole new avenues for innovation open up and shared value is created. Society's gains are even greater because businesses could be far more effective than governments and not-for-profit organisations at persuading customers to embrace products and services that create social benefits.

However, given the context of today's conference, it is also important to highlight that Porter and Kramer have extended the idea of shared value to not-for-profits and governments and they argue that this concept blurs the line between for-profit and not-for-profit organisations[21]. They also suggest that governments and NGOs will be most effective if they think in value terms – considering benefit relative to costs – and focus on the results achieved rather than the funds and effort expended.

They argue that the principle of shared value creation cuts across the traditional divide between the responsibilities of business and those of government or civil society. It doesn't matter what type of organisation creates the value. What matters is that benefits are delivered by those organisations or combinations of organisations that are best positioned to achieve the most impact for the least cost. Finding ways to boost productivity and innovation is equally valuable in the pursuit of commercial or social objectives.

The market economy is an unrivalled vehicle for meeting human needs, improving efficiency, creating jobs and building wealth. But a narrow conception of capitalism has prevented business from harnessing its full potential to meet society's broader challenges. We need a more sophisticated form of capitalism, one imbued with a social purpose. But it is completely unrealistic to suggest that a theoretical notion of shared social responsibilities is the most powerful force for addressing the pressing issues that society faces. This should come from a deeper understanding of competition and economic value creation.

---

[21] Porter, M.E. and Kramer, M.R., 2010. Creating Shared Value: How to fix capitalism. Harvard Business Review, December 2010.

5.
Intergenerational Solidarity and its Role in Shaping the Future

Mary Cunningham

Introduction

Increased life expectancy is the good news story of the 20th century; we experienced a greater extension of years during that period than in the previous five thousand years. This demographic evolution will be accompanied by profound social change.

The current crisis is further sharpening the sense of urgency for us to review fundamentally the way our society functions. Some groups have been particularly badly hit by the crisis, including the young, the low skilled, children in unemployed households, migrant workers, ethnic minorities and older people. Services provided by and commissioned on behalf of the state are faced with unprecedented financial challenges and major changes are being introduced at all levels to cut public spending. The long term social impact of what has happened in Ireland is still to emerge.

Changes in the economy and in the family are intertwined both positively and negatively. It is critical that those with responsibility for implementing the changes are acutely aware of the needs of the more vulnerable and regard social policies as a long term investment rather than just a cost to the public purse. Commentators have often referred to Ireland as being much more than just an economy. They have argued that we are a society as well, indeed going further in stating that society and economy are two sides of the same coin.

Challenges

Many changes in our society – such as geographic mobility- have led to generations frequently becoming segregated from one another – especially younger and older people. This separation can lead to unrealistic, negative stereotypes of whole generations and a decrease in positive exchanges between them. Yet these separated generations do have resources of value to each other and share areas of concern, for example, both younger and older generations are often marginalised in decision-making that directly affects their lives. Both also are subjected to negative stereotyping, sometimes towards each other.

The 2006 census recorded that there were 462,000 people aged 65+ living in Ireland; this is 11% of the population. Looking to the future, recent research[22] projected that there will be 1.4 million people aged 65+ in 2041, making up more than 22% of the total population.

The debate so far is too often focused on the negative challenges of ageing, such as the need for increased expenditure on pensions, health care and social protection. It is important that this emerging situation is not seen in just strictly financial terms, such changes impose challenges on us all and requires us to explore approaches based on solidarity between the generations as a more sustainable way forward for a more equal and fair society, especially in a period of crisis.

It is critical that these challenges are addressed within a framework of enhanced solidarity and mutual co-operation. A shared and better understanding of new forms of co-existence between generations is necessary to avoid situations where they are presented as a conflict between young and older people.

These demographic changes put at stake the sustainability of the current pensions systems, which affects people from all generations and will have

---

[22] Mc Gill, Paul. Illustrating Ageing in Ireland North and South: Key Facts and Figures. Belfast: Centre for Ageing Research and Development in Ireland. 2010.

most affect on people in decades to come. Additionally, younger people are also facing the growing challenge of reconciling their working life, their family life whilst providing support for the older people in their families.

An approach which promotes greater social cohesion can play a key role in developing fairer and more sustainable responses to the major economic and social challenges that we're facing. Ireland is lagging behind in this regard. We need to be genuinely and sincerely more inclusive to enable everyone to get involved, building on the positive resources that the young and old have to offer each other and those around them.

Opportunities

There are many potential opportunities that can be harnessed as a result of enhanced intergenerational solidarity. One of the main benefits of greater intergenerational solidarity is the promotion of more cohesive communities. It has the potential to bridge the gap between generations and to allow younger people to learn from older people, the values, experience and knowledge acquired through life can be passed on while older people can benefit from young people's recently acquired and updated knowledge, the area of IT is an excellent example. Young people can also share their energy, vitality, commitment and optimism.

Why is this shared understanding and learning between generations so important?

The status quo in Ireland, has meant that in reality it is okay to exclude almost one sixth of the population from the mainstream of the life of the society, while substantial resources and opportunities are channelled towards other groups in society[23] .The sharing of social responsibilities is an alternative to the status quo which, through the involvement of all stakeholders, both strong and weak, will give rise to common and sustainable solutions, fully acknowledging their contributions and

---
[23] Social Justice Ireland: An Agenda for a New Ireland. Socio Economic Review 2010

legitimate aspirations. We need to create a society for all. The promotion of intergenerational solidarity serves to bridge this divide and alleviate the inequality so often prevalent in Irish society.

The draft Council of Europe Charter identifies Shared Social Responsibilities as a means of securing social, environmental and intergenerational justice. It places future generations and their possibilities for development at the heart of present day decisions. The Charter encourages all stakeholders, governments, business, financial sectors, trade unions, civil society organisations, media, education, families and individuals to fully participate in the sharing of social responsibilities.

What needs to happen?

Intergenerational issues arise in most areas of public policy. It isn't and shouldn't be limited to discussions on pensions and long term care. Intergenerational solidarity needs to be developed and embedded at both a policy and a practice level: -

- Policies need to strengthen intergenerational solidarity and unite generations;
- Involve young people and older people in political processes that affect their rights;
- Exchange good practices and mutual learning between different generations;
- Provide intergenerational activities in schools and communities;
- Encourage older people to become role models for active ageing and to mentor young people;
- Initiatives need to be developed that support intergenerational contact;
- Promote and provide life-long learning opportunities;
- Identify spaces in communities that facilitate social interaction and interdependence among young and old;
- Recognise the value of volunteering and expand opportunities for young and old to participate in meaningful volunteer activities;

- Recognise and support the important role of grandparents;
- Consider the establishment of an intergenerational council of elders and young people to advise Government on policy;
- Foster co-operation among NGOs that work with children, young people and older people;
- Work with the media to provide realistic and positive images of young people and older people;

Conclusion

Intergenerational Solidarity means different things to different people. To some, it simply means that different age groups have a positive view of one another, which raises the important issue of the degree to and the way in which different generations interact. Others stress the importance of consensus between generations on the best way forward. I believe that it needs to be both of these in order to reduce the marginalisation of both young and old. Intergenerational solidarity is under threat. Social and economic changes may endanger it. We need to make conscious efforts to foster intergenerational solidarity.

The challenge that now faces us is one of building that real alternative, one that sees the economy as an instrument of social inclusion, of social harmony; we must acknowledge new challenges such as the need for intergenerational solidarity that requires us to build sustainability into all policies. If we don't intergenerational solidarity may break down and then we all will lose out.

6.
Sharing Responsibility in Shaping the Future: An Environmental Perspective

Participatory Democracy - The Story of a Trojan Horse

Michael Ewing

1. The Gestation and Birth of the Aarhus Convention

2012 sees the 20th anniversary of Ireland's commitment to environmental participatory democracy in signing the "Rio Declaration on Environment and Development"[24] of 1992. Principle 10 of the Declaration reads:

> Environmental issues are best handled with participation of all concerned citizens, at the relevant level. At the national level, each individual shall have appropriate access to information concerning the environment that is held by public authorities, including information on hazardous materials and activities in their communities, and the opportunity to participate in decision-making processes. States shall facilitate and encourage public awareness and participation by making information widely available. Effective access to judicial and administrative proceedings, including redress and remedy, shall be provided.

This tenth Principle was to be the beginning of a quiet human rights revolution and, as will be seen, its offspring are still evolving across the globe. The first major step in its propagation was made in Europe, where

---

[24] http://www.unep.org/Documents.Multilingual/Default.asp?documentid=78&articleid=1163 [Accessed 10/08/2011]

European environmental NGOs, realising the significance of this aspirational statement, worked together with the governments of the UNECE[25] to produce an international convention in Aarhus in 2008. This raised Principle 10 from an inspirational aspiration to the status of a legally binding treaty known as the Aarhus Convention[26]. The objective of the Convention is made absolutely clear in Article 1:

> In order to contribute to the protection of the right of every person of present and future generations to live in an environment adequate to his or her health and well-being, each Party shall guarantee the rights of access to information, public participation in decision-making, and access to justice in environmental matters in accordance with the provisions of this Convention.
>
> Although regional in scope the significance of the Aarhus Convention is global. It is by far the most impressive elaboration of Principle 10 of the Rio Declaration, which stresses the need for citizens' participation in environmental issues and for access to information on the environment held by public authorities. As such it is the most ambitious venture in the area of environmental democracy so far undertaken under the auspices of the United Nations.
>
> Kofi Annan, United Nations Secretary-General (1997-2008)

Ireland was one of the 40 signatories to the Convention. At the time of writing, some 13 years later, Ireland remains the only one of the EU 27 not to ratify the Convention, denying the public on this part of the island of Ireland protection regarding the following three fundamental rights contained therein.

---

[25] United Nations Economic Commission for Europe.
http://www.unece.org/Welcome.html [Accessed 10/08/2011]

[26] The UNECE "Convention on Access to Information, Public Participation in Decision-making and Access to Justice in Environmental Matters" was adopted on 25th June 1998 in the Danish city of Aarhus at the Fourth Ministerial Conference in the 'Environment for Europe' process.
http://live.unece.org/env/pp/welcome.html [Accessed 10/08/2011]

- The right of access to information on the environment
- The right to participate in decision-making affecting their health or the environment
- The right to have access to justice when these rights are denied or when acts and omissions by private individuals and public authorities contravene provisions of national law relating to the environment

2. Participatory Democracy and the Convention

This relatively short international legal instrument places clear obligations on the Parties to ensure greater public participation in environmental issues and easy access to justice if these rights are denied. It calls for effective dissemination of environmental information as well as greater transparency in decision-making procedures. This will lead to more information being made available, which in turn will make for better decision-making and a healthier environment. This Convention marked a new chapter in preserving the environment but also in further strengthening democracy.

One simple way of visualising the convention is as a three-legged stool. All three legs need to be well-crafted and of solid construction for the stool to be of any use. Without a right to have access to information it is impossible to participate effectively in decision-making. Without easily accessible, timely, effective and inexpensive access to justice it is not possible for the public to uphold the other two rights. Without proactive dissemination of information regarding these rights, the public will not even know they exist.

Principle 10 and its daughter Convention provide a foundation for building a sustainable future for humanity. Without a well-informed and engaged public, the many serious and difficult decisions that need to be made, for example to avoid cataclysmic climate change, will never be made until it is too late. The Convention also: clearly links environmental rights and human rights; acknowledges that we owe an obligation to future generations; establishes that sustainable development can be achieved only through the involvement of all stakeholders; links government accountability and environmental protection; and focuses on interactions between the public and public authorities in a democratic context.

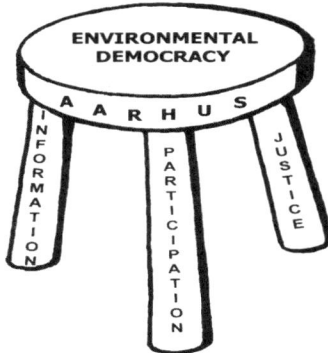

The Three Legged Convention

3. The European Union, the Aarhus Convention and Ireland

The European Union ratified the Convention in 2005, and this had its knock on effect in Ireland, because in order to ratify, the EU had to put its own legislative house in order. This meant ensuring that all environmental Directives to the Member States were in line with the Convention and that it issued new Directives to prescribe for the three pillars of the Convention. Three new directives were developed: one on access to information[27]; one on public participation[28], amending a

---

[27] DIRECTIVE 2003/4/EC OF THE EUROPEAN PARLIAMENT AND OF THE COUNCIL
of 28 January 2003 on public access to environmental information and repealing Council Directive 90/313/EEC
http://eur-lex.europa.eu/LexUriServ/LexUriServ.do?uri=OJ:L:2003:041:0026:0032:EN:PDF [Accessed 10/08/2011]

number of existing important environmental directives; and one providing for access to justice.[29] The first two Directives came into effect in 2003, the last one remains at the level of a proposal due to an apparent reluctance to complete the realisation of the Convention's potential.

It seems that although all the EU Member States and the EU itself, signed and, with the exception of Ireland, ratified the Convention, it was only later that they understood the "Trojan Horse" that they had created. Whatever about giving people on-paper rights to participate in decision-making, the idea of enabling them to enforce those rights was a step too far, and the Member States left this elegant blueprint for participatory democracy parked at front of the gates of the European Union.

However all is not lost regarding access to justice, in that the Convention itself provides a unique mechanism where any person, anywhere on the planet can approach the Aarhus Convention Compliance Committee (ACCC)[30], even regarding another country (i.e. not the country of residence/citizenship) as long as that country is a Party to the Convention. A "communication" is submitted to the ACCC explaining why it is thought that a specific country is in non-compliance with the Convention. This is called a "public trigger", and leads to a problem solving process where the

---

[28] DIRECTIVE 2003/35/EC OF THE EUROPEAN PARLIAMENT AND OF THE COUNCIL
of 26 May 2003 providing for public participation in respect of the drawing up of certain plans and programmes relating to the environment and amending with regard to public participation and access to justice Council Directives 85/337/EEC and 96/61/EC
http://eur-lex.europa.eu/LexUriServ/LexUriServ.do?uri=OJ:L:2003:156:0017:0024:EN:PDF [Accessed 10/08/2011]

[29] This proposed directive grants citizens the right to initiate administrative or judicial procedures against acts or omissions that do not comply with environmental law. It is also intended to implement at the level of the Community and the Member States the third pillar of the Convention The ultimate aim is to improve the application of environmental law.
http://europa.eu/legislation_summaries/environment/general_provisions/l28141_en.htm [Accessed 10/08/2011]

[30] http://www.participate.org/index.php?option=com_content&view=article&id=162&Itemid=223 [Accessed 10/08/2011]

communicant and the Party in question are treated as equal voices and a resolution is sought through an exchange initially by letter and then in a public hearing or hearings where the communicant and the Party sit with the ACCC and try to get a resolution that will ensure that the Party concerned moves to become compliant. Anyone can participate in the meetings of the Committee (as observer) and even speak. The only exception is the very last stage of developing findings and recommendations when the meeting is closed to all except the Committee. The use of the "public trigger" enables advocacy on behalf of the public in Parties where local civil society is under duress. That said recent several recent cases focus on both access to the European Court of Justice and, perhaps of particular interest to Ireland considering our closely related legal systems, access to justice in the UK[31].

4. Ireland and the Convention

So bearing in mind our membership of the EU, the Treaty of Rome and the Vienna Convention on the Law of Treaties[32] how do we fare in Ireland in terms of the aspirations of the Convention and Principle 10[33]? The following three sections try to answer this question.

i Access to information – the foundation for building participatory democracy

Directive 2003/4/EC was finally transposed into Irish law in 2007 as the Access to Information on the Environment Regulations SI. No 133 of 2007[34]. These AIE Regulations provide: a mechanism more far-reaching than the Freedom of Information Acts as it includes all "public authorities"

---

[31] http://doku.cac.at/accc2011_rel.pdf [Accessed 10/08/2011]
[32] http://untreaty.un.org/ilc/texts/instruments/english/conventions/1_1_1969.pdf [Accessed 10/08/2011]
[33] The Treaty of Rome states that Member States are subject to EU law and to any international treaties entered into by the EU. The Vienna Convention states that signatories to Conventions must have regard to the provisions of the convention and at least not do anything to diminish its provisions.
[34] http://www.attorneygeneral.ie/esi/2007/B25144.pdf [Accessed 10/08/2011]

including semi-state bodies; access to information at little or no cost within one month of the request; a two stage administrative appeals mechanism, the first stage being at no cost the second costing €150; and the establishment of the office of the Commissioner for Environmental Information[35]. Apart from the appeal fee, which the Commissioner herself recommends should be removed, the normative and organisational aspects of the transposition phase for implementing the Directive still require some tweaking to be in line with the spirit of the Convention. However, as is so often the case in the implementation of EU Environmental Directives, the operational phase[36] of implementation is very poor. Very few people, even those working in the environmental area, have been trained in their operation, or in many cases even know that these regulations and the concomitant rights exist. Such is the priority given to the proactive dissemination of information on the environment!

A number of requests for information have been denied by public authorities under these AIE regulations and some of these have been appealed to the Commissioner. One in particular is deserving of a mention here. This relates to a request for information from the Department of the Taoiseach in 2007.[37] Mr Gary Fitzgerald BL made a request for copies of Cabinet papers relating to a discussion in Cabinet regarding greenhouse gas emissions on the basis that Directive 2003/4/EC does not allow for exemptions when it comes to information regarding the release of emissions to the environment. This request was refused on internal appeal by the Department. The Commissioner then made a decision that the relevant information should be handed over. This was appealed by the Department to the High Court who upheld the decision of the Commissioner. The Department has now appealed this to the Supreme Court.

---

[35] http://www.ocei.gov.ie/en/ [Accessed 10/08/2011]

[36] Treaty of Rome, *Article 10 EC. Member States shall take all appropriate measures, whether general or particular, to ensure fulfilment of the obligations arising out of this Treaty or resulting from action taken by the institutions of the Community. They shall facilitate the achievement of the Community's tasks.*

[37] http://www.ocei.gov.ie/en/DecisionsoftheCommissioner/Name,8962,en.htm [Accessed 10/08/2011]

The other worrying aspect regarding the implementation of this pillar of the Convention is the manner in which information is stored and made available. Whilst there are examples of good practice there are also sadly many poor ones. The Public are entitled to know what is happening to the environment and should be able to rely on the various public authorities to proactively, and as appropriate reactively, provide them with the timely information that they need to protect their health and the environment and in a manner that they can easily access and digest it. It is not an overly complex process to convert emissions data into easily understood live online information.

ii. Public Participation – The Heart of the Convention

At the heart of the Convention is the involvement of the public in environmental decision-making (EDM). Traditionally in Ireland, in EDM as in a lot of other areas of decision-making, the norm was either "Decide, Announce and Defend" (DAD) or perhaps the more cynical "Decide Educate, Announce and Defend" (DEAD). Here the problem holder/decision-making authority just informs the public of a previously made decision and asking for comments, which may or may not be heeded. The Convention goes well beyond this, requiring real participation at the earliest possible moment.

> *Article 5.4. Each Party shall provide for early public participation, when all options are open and effective public participation can take place.*

The Convention provides that public participation should be timely, effective, adequate and formal, and contain information, notification, dialogue, consideration, and response.

When talking about public participation in EDM it is important to understand to what we refer. Who are the 'public'? What is 'participation'? What are the 'decisions' to which it refers?

Starting with the last and working backwards, EDM refers to any process of decision-making where consequent significant environmental impacts are a possibility. This includes law making, policy making, land use planning, strategic planning, resource management planning, licensing of industry, environmental assessment, spatial planning, budgetary decisions etc. These are all provided for in the Convention.

It should also be noted that EDM can be even more complex than decision-making on other public issues. First, environmental impacts do not respect property, jurisdiction or boundaries. Second, EDM can involve government agencies as both manager and regulator. Thirdly, environmental issues can provide especially heated value conflicts that require value trade-offs.[38]

Given the need to overcome these complexities it is clear that participatory decision-making leads to better outputs that are more widely accepted and owned and that the process will generally be shorter and less costly as illustrated below.

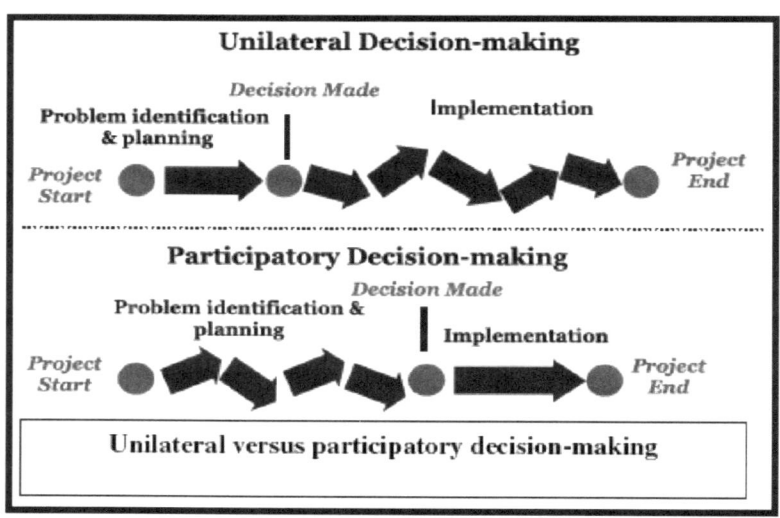

Unilateral versus participatory decision-making

---

[38] Dale M, H. English M, R. (1999). *Tools to Aid Environmental Decision-Making*. Springer. P.9.

"Participatory decision-making processes usually take much more time than unilateral decision-making. However, as illustrated in this figure, this is usually more than offset by time gains (and, by implication, effectiveness) in the implementation phase." [39]

Participation for sustainability is also important in recognising the value and relevance of local knowledge.[40] If properly undertaken this means that local knowledge is part of the decision making process, and weighed up with knowledge from other sources, solutions are developed relevant to that community, rather than being imposed by external experts. We have only to look at the chaos in Rossport, Co Mayo resulting from the use of a DEAD process to see how important this is.

Simply stated then, to participate is to take part, to share and act together. But clearly, as practiced, public participation means different things to different people. In this context it is useful to look at "Arnstein's ladder" (illustrated below). Arnstein represents the levels of public participation as the 8 rungs of a ladder and groups the rungs into three groups. The continuum stretches from going through the empty ritual of non-participation, to having the real power needed to affect the outcome of the process. Arnstein describes this first category non-participation as tactics whose real objective is "to enable power holders to educate, or cure the participants". In the degrees of tokenism Arnstein argues that when these are "proffered by power holders as the total extent of participation, citizens may indeed hear and be heard. But they lack the power to ensure that they are heeded".

So when the Convention requires public participation it is a process that enables the public to know that its voice has been heard and heeded, even when dealing with national as opposed to local issues. This requires the development of new and more inclusive ways of having conversations.

---

[39] Ridder, Mostert, Wolters, (2005) *Harmonising Collaborative Planning (HarmoniCOP); Learning Together to Manage Together/Improving Participation in Water Management*

[40] Fien, J., Scott, W. & Tilbury, D. (2002) *Exploring Principles of Good Practice: Learning from a metaanalysis of case studies on education within conservation across the WWF network.* Applied Environmental Education and Communication, 1: p. 153-162.

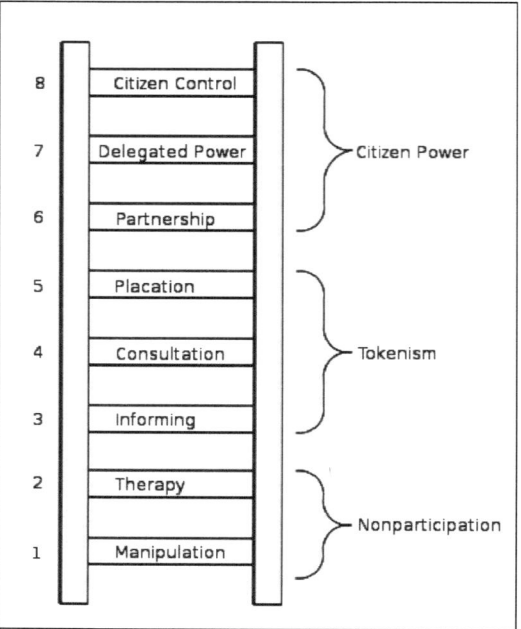

Diagram Arnstein's Ladder[41]

What then is 'the public'? The public is often treated as a unitary body, whereas in reality it is a collection of numerous continually shifting interests and alliances[42], which may be in conflict with each other. The term is used as a "catch-all to describe those with an interest in a decision, other than a proponent, operator, or responsible authority".[43] The individuals making up a public may be involved as individuals or as members of organisations. They may become involved due to their proximity, economics, social or environmental issues, values, etc.

---

[41] Arnstein, Sherry R. "A Ladder of Citizen Participation," JAIP, Vol. 35, No. 4, July 1969, pp. 216-224.

[42] Ortolano, L. (1997) *Environmental Regulations And Impact Assessment.* John Wiley & Sons 402-422.

[43] Petts, J. and Leach, B. (2000) *Evaluating Methods for Public Participation: Literature Review.* R & D Technical Report E135. Environment Agency. UK.

By contrast, stakeholders, of which the public is one, are literally those with a stake in an issue and may include non-governmental organizations (NGO's), government or its agents, industry, individuals, communities etc. Stakeholders do not always want to be involved in an EDM process, but they have the right to know, if their interests are affected. They may want to become involved at a different stage of the EDM process.

Research by Ewing[44] and more recently by Kelly[45] and others would indicate a serious gap in understanding and trust between stakeholders. The question then must be asked as to the cause of this mistrust, and what methods can we use to diminish it. Laurian[46] finds that this lack of trust is greater in low income communities and consequently they are less likely to participate in decision-making processes. Sudulich[47] supports this assertion, and continues:

> From a brief overview of the concept of democracy, it should be clear that democracy and effective public participation have not been always a natural pair. Some forms and concepts of democracy are devoid of considerations for participative elements, and participation reduced to voting has been dominant for a long time. At present, however, we are witnessing a fundamental change, both in the theoretical conceptualisation of democracy and in its practical exercise. If democracy and participation have not always gone together, it seems that today both want to be united again.

---

[44] Ewing, M.K. (2003). *Public Participation in Environmental Decision-making*. 80-112 http://gdrc.org/decision/participation-edm.html [Accessed 10/08/2011]

[45] Kelly, M. (2007). *Environmental Debates and the Public in Ireland*. IPA. 209-215

[46] Laurian, L (2004) *Public participation in environmental decision making - Findings from communities facing toxic waste cleanup*, JOURNAL OF THE AMERICAN PLANNING ASSOCIATION, 70 (1): 53-65 WIN 2004 ISSN: 0194-4363

[47] Sudulich, M,L, *Participatory Democracy. An Evolving Concept and its Potential for Youth Involvement*   http://www.google.com/search?q=cache:qjmMNxevxG4J: www.tcd.ie/Political_Science/Postgrads/Laura_Sudulich/YouthPoliticalParticipation .doc+Constitution+of+NGO&hl=en&gl=ie&ct=clnk&cd=12 [Accessed 10/08/2011]

In a similar vein, following its researches, the Taskforce on Active Citizenship highlighted the following issues[48]:

- A perceived democratic deficit especially but not exclusively at the local level where some communities and citizens feel powerless to influence decisions about planning, public services and other areas;
- A low level of participation in politics, community organisations, volunteering or neighbourhood activities driven by personal choice or forced economic circumstances;
- A risk of social fragmentation or rift where the better-off can buy out of the public sphere and into private health, education, leisure and gated communities etc.; and
- A lack of appropriate structures in which citizens – all citizens – can debate with others on matters of common concern; listen to other points of view; come to agreements and take appropriate action.

To be part of the decision-making process, to feel part of the establishment increases the level of people's identification with political institutions. In fact, the other main benefit generated by the participatory method in civil and political life is an increase in people's trust in institutions. A good example is the case of Porto Alegre, the first and most advanced experience of participation at local level, which resulted in a significant increase in people's confidence in the establishment. Porto Alegre's experience started in 1989, when the "Administracao Popular" implanted a form of Participative Budget; every year, an average of 45,000 people meet in several types of assemblies in order to discuss it.

Groups and organisations working together towards a decision/outcome, like relationships, go through recognisable stages[49]. The early stages have been described as:

---

[48] The Concept of Active Citizenship.(2007)
http://www.aughty.org/pdf/activecitizen.pdf [Accessed 10/8/2011]

[49] Bruce Tuckman's 1965 Forming Storming Norming Performing team-development model
http://www.businessballs.com/tuckmanformingstormingnormingperforming.htm [Accessed 10/8/2011]

- Forming: coming together as a group, getting to know each other, deciding what the group's concerns and emphases should be.
- Storming: coming to terms with differences within the group.
- Norming: agreeing objectives, priorities, procedures, and ways of relating to each other.
- Performing: getting on with the work, without having to spend a lot of time and energy deciding what needs doing and how it should be done.

All of this is difficult enough in a group which meets frequently, or in a formal organisation. It should be no surprise that it is even more complex in a participation process when so many different interests have to find a common vision. The involvement of skilled well trained facilitators/dialogue planners can create the right circumstances for creative dialogue in most situations. However, extensive research is also needed to develop new tools that enable creative and honest conversations that lead to widely owned and effective outcomes from decision-making processes, including appropriate alternative dispute resolution (ADR) techniques. The need for these skills and for a wider societal understanding of new ways of dialogue will become increasingly more important as the demand for diminishing natural resources meets the rapidly growing needs of a burgeoning world population.

In the meantime the following should be adopted as the fundamentals of public participation processes at all levels of governance.[50]

1. The public participation process seeks out and facilitates the participation of those potentially affected
2. The public is involved in how they will participate
3. There are multiple methods for participation

---

[50] Ridder, Mostert, Wolters, "*Harmonising Collaborative Planning (HarmoniCOP); Learning Together to Manage Together/Improving Participation in Water Management*"; 2005 (*From "Public Involvement Needs Assessment, Appendix H, Centre for Collaborative Study, 2005)*

4. The venues for public participation are accessible to the diverse public
5. The PP process provides participants with the information they need to participate in a meaningful way.
6. Methods for participation are user-friendly and perceived as fair, just and respectful
7. Public's role in decision-making is clear from the outset
8. The public's contribution has the potential to meaningfully influence the decision or outcomes
9. The PP process communicates to participants how their input affected the decision or outcomes
10. The public has the opportunity to be involved and/or monitor the implementation of the decision or outcomes

iii. Access to Justice –
"The law, in its majestic equality, forbids the rich, as well as the poor, to sleep under the bridges, to beg in the streets, and to steal bread".
Anatole France[51]

Of all the three legs of the three-legged stool illustrated above, this is by far the most broken, though not necessarily the most difficult to fix. Like the legendary Ritz Hotel anyone can enter the Irish Judicial system but only those with deep pockets can afford to stay there. This is clearly not unique to matters environmental, and the potential for change created by the provisions of the Convention could create precedence for the public trying to assert other rights within this republic. But it is not just in the judicial system where the public seek justice. Administrative processes such as the planning appeals process also need an overhaul to enable equal access.

Under the Convention access-to-justice procedures must be fair, equitable, timely and not prohibitively expensive. They must also provide adequate and effective remedies and be carried out by independent and

---

[51] http://www.aphorismsgalore.com/author/Anatole_France.html. [Accessed 10/8/2011]   Anatole France (1844-1924) won the Nobel Prize in 1921.

impartial bodies. The Convention also requires information on access-to-justice procedures to be disseminated and encourages the development of assistance mechanisms to remove or reduce financial and other barriers.

Comparing the effectiveness, humanity and equitable nature of the Aarhus Convention Compliance Committee with the experiences of many in engaging with administrative bodies in Ireland, allows us to see what might be possible. The Irish planning process for example is so complex that in many cases participants feel that they cannot represent themselves and find it necessary to obtain legal and expert advice from the very beginning at earliest stages. The equality of arms implied in Article 6 of the European Charter of Human Rights is largely absent here as it often is in the judicial system, even where legal aid is provided. Legal aid is not available to those fighting what are often public interest environmental cases, neither is support available under the Voluntary Assistance Scheme of the Bar Council.

The broad range of legal remedies available in cases of environmental issues are undermined by the cost of taking cases through the courts system, and reform in the area of cost shifting measures and the encouragement of Public Interest Law in Ireland are vital to counteracting this.

Apart from the complexities of the costs issues that would discourage everyone but the very rich or the very determined pauper from engaging with the judicial system, delay is also a fact of life in the Irish Courts system, with cases taking years to process. A striking example of which is the fourteen year legal battle that occurred in the case of Rooney v An Bord Pleanála[52] concerning the attempts by one Declan Rooney to prosecute Galway County Council for opening and keeping an illegal dump at Carrowbrowne, Galway, County Galway, near his home.

---

[52] Rooney v An Bord Pleanala [2003] IEHC 100 (20 March 2003)

Many barriers were encountered and even though Galway County Council were found to be manifestly in breach of planning conditions on several occasions during this fourteen year legal battle, they fought the case strongly to avoid liability. Mr Rooney faced financial ruin at many points during this lengthy process. This is not an enabling atmosphere in which members of the public are encouraged to enforce the law of the state through "active citizenship". In any democracy the citizens should be able to call those in power to task if they exceed their powers or contravene the laws of the state, and in cases which involve environmental harm, delay can be fatal, as once environmental damage occurs it is often difficult, if not impossible to reverse. The establishment of an "Environment List" in the courts would like the "Commercial Court List" enable a faster access to justice where the precautionary principle[53] makes this essential. It is a measure of the perverse value system embraced by this society that decisions to protect the resources that provide the fundamentals of life are considered to be so much less important than money.

The right of individuals and NGOs to bring cases (the right to standing) is also a very problematic area and one that needs serious attention by Government as required under the Convention.

One other important issue which needs to be addressed is the issue of capacity building of members of the public with regard to their rights and how to exercise them. Individual members of the public are at the frontline when it comes to environmental issues, but unless they know what their rights are and understand how to use the various channels available to exercise them, these rights are rendered meaningless. NGOs and grassroots environmental organisations have an important role to play in developing awareness of rights and their infringements and in assisting

---

[53] Principle 15 of the Rio Declaration: "In order to protect the environment, the precautionary approach shall be widely applied by States according to their capabilities. Where there are threats of serious or irreversible damage, lack of full scientific certainty shall not be used as a reason for postponing cost-effective measures to prevent environmental degradation." As applied to environmental policy, the precautionary principle stipulates that for practices such as the release of radiation or toxins or massive deforestation the burden of proof lies with the advocates.

people in asserting their rights. NGOs should be given support in this role as required under the Convention as they can often be more effective in this than public authorities.

> Article 3.4. Each Party shall provide for appropriate recognition of and support to associations, organizations or groups promoting environmental protection and ensure that its national legal system is consistent with this obligation.

There are clearly serious issues regarding Access to Justice in Ireland which require urgent attention if the goal of achieving sustainable development and providing a clean and healthy environment for all citizens is to be a realistic one.

5. The Current Situation Regarding Ratification

Ratification of the Aarhus Convention was a part of the Programme for Government (PFG) under the previous Fianna Fail/Green Party Government and is also part of the current PFG. The recently passed Environment (Miscellaneous Provisions) Act 2011 provides the final necessary legislative changes in Part 2 to enable ratification of the Convention. Following the commencement of Part 2 the technical process of ratification can proceed. Hopefully this will be before the end of 2011.

90 days after ratification the Convention will come into effect in Ireland and one year after that it will be open to anyone to make a "communication" to the ACCC.

Apart from ratification of the Convention, an important first step in its implementation is to amend the Irish Constitution in order *recognise the right of every person of present and future generations to live in an environment adequate to his or her health and well-being*, as set out in Article 1, the objective of the Convention.

6. The Trojan Horse and Participatory Democracy

Hopefully the last few pages have given some indication of the potential of the Convention as a change-making treaty, as well as how much this change is needed in Ireland as elsewhere. Internationally it has already created waves in the governance of both the Western Europe Parties and the Aarhus Parties from the former Soviet Union. On an even wider scale, the United Nations Environment Programme (UNEP) is following up on the success of the Aarhus Convention by leading a move to develop either a new treaty designed to bring about the implementation of Principle 10 globally, or a series of regional treaties, with South America poised to be the first to go down this road.

The Convention has another dimension in that it requires the Parties to promote the principles of the Convention in all international fora. This has great potential for change in the sometimes chaotic UNFCC processes and other conventions and treaties that are less than embracing of civil society input.

Its potential for changing the way we do business here in Ireland at local, regional and national levels is enormous, but it will require champions for participatory democracy to open the gates and allow the Trojan Horse into the citadel that is our decaying representative democracy. The ratification of the Convention is only the beginning of a journey to bring the participatory democratic processes that are essential if we are to respond to the environmental challenges that we have created for ourselves. The need to focus on reversing the decline in the well-being of the planet alongside that of the human race will require the active involvement of all. The Aarhus Convention is a valuable tool to be used in starting that conversation.

7.
Sharing Responsibility to Maximize Positive Outcomes: Co-Production, Community Participation and Public Services

Ivan Cooper

Community participation in co-producing public services will ensure best outcomes in developing people's capabilities

Ireland faces many challenges to deliver a sustainable social and economic recovery. Reforming how we fund and deliver our public services is now generally accepted as being critical to recovery: if we can deliver reform that puts the citizen at the centre of both the design and delivery of joined up, personalised public services then we will get maximum value for money and the best possible outcomes from our limited resources. Public services are delivered by both public sector and community and voluntary organisations, and both sets of actors have big roles to play in delivering the reforms required.

It's all about outcomes

Delivering the best possible outcome in a person's life should be the aim of all services, but particularly of our public services. Outcomes are experienced in people's lives and are a product of the interaction between the persons' need and the effectiveness of the service in meeting that need. Positive outcomes are the improvements in quality of life that a good service brings about.

Only the person benefiting from a service can truly know whether the service is meeting their need and how the service could be improved to better meet that need. Delivering the best possible outcome for a person or a community involves that person or community being able to secure for themselves - from public resources when appropriate - the service they determine is required to meet their need. That means people having an adequate choice of service configurations *or* control over the specific service they require, and ideally means both.

If providing choice is impractical then providing control is essential. Control means being able to direct the service, within practical constraints that should be recognised and agreed by users. Service-users must therefore be able to shape both the design and implementation of the service being offered if the best possible outcomes are to be delivered.

This is the essence of the *co-production approach* that *puts the person at the heart of public services.* The approach involves much more than simple consulting. It demands that public-service-providers be directed by, and be answerable to, service users. There is a big advocacy and support role for community and voluntary organisations here. It demands service users having a full understanding of their own needs and of the resource-constraints to be taken into account in delivering the required service. It demands service users being able, and being supported, to shape and control the design and implementation of the services they require.

Achieving outcome-focussed public services will therefore require a significant re-design of the structures and processes we generally use to deliver public services. The current crisis presents a once-in-a-generation opportunity to reform public services to put people at the heart of personalised services, tailored to individual need (rather than a one-size fits all approach) that they themselves are involved in designing and monitoring.

Achieving this will require:

- Delegating authority for controlling tailored public services to local communities and to supported service-users. The responsibility to fund and ensure the availability and adequacy of those services must remain clearly with the state.
- It does not mean dumping responsibility on local communities and

individual service-users without sufficient public resources being available.
- Changing the whole approach to public budget setting and tax-resource allocation, with new participatory approaches being developed at all levels of government, and particularly at the community level where services should ideally be designed, delivered, monitored and governed.
- Elected public representatives recognising that it is not their role to directly provide everything for the communities that elected them. Their role is to ensure communities are supported and empowered to provide for themselves using adequate public resources made available for that purpose.
- Conversely this will mean much greater levels of responsibility being accepted locally, and comprehensive statutory supports provided to assist voluntary-and-community-led governance and local/person-centred service provision.

We also need to nurture a greater sense of obligation by individuals to the members of their communities of place and interest to participate in the work of organising community and public services.

Sharing responsibility to maximise positive outcomes

Sharing responsibility in shaping the future is a big theme, about as big as they come. Importantly the theme is expressed in the present continuous and suggests that we are all participating – actively or passively - in shaping the future, whether we are aware of it or not. The challenge essentially consists in each of us accepting our duty to become more actively involved in contributing in whatever way we can to envisioning and sustaining the society that we want to live in. We have delegated that role to professional politicians for too long.

The theme begs the question as to whether we are effectively sharing responsibility in shaping the future, and if not how we can better share that responsibility. Are each of us playing our part in shaping the future to maximise positive outcomes for ourselves, our families, and our communities; local, national and international? And if not, what can we do to maximise our participation in shaping our collective futures to deliver the best possible outcomes?

Clearly this theme is truly all-encompassing so this paper will approach the theme from the perspective of community participation in the co-production (planning and monitoring) of public services aimed at developing people's capabilities.

I will argue that by becoming involved in community and voluntary activity we give expression to our willingness to share responsibility with each other in shaping the future for ourselves, our families, our communities and indeed for the national and international communities we are a part of. In effect, we become trustees and guardians for each other.

I will also argue that when community and voluntary activity is adequately supported by public funds it:

- nurtures and gives expression to the duty of care that we have towards one another and builds a sense of citizenship; enables us to cooperate in devising and delivering a shared vision and co-produced solutions (in the form of positive outcomes) to collectively identified community needs;
- enables delivery of person-centred public services to deliver outcomes that develop people's capabilities

Major themes in co-production

Simply attempting to reduce the cost of the way we currently deliver public services and aiming to do the same things cheaper may reduce the short term deficit but will not deliver the long term reforms that are both required and possible. We should recognise that all people have capabilities which it is the duty of society, through the collaborative efforts of the state and communities of citizens, to nurture and develop. It starts there and is as simple as that.

If we start with a clear vision that we want our public services to develop our capabilities and those of our families, friends, colleagues and society as a whole, then we will see that - like taking a strategic approach to any challenge – it will mean involving and resourcing citizens to take ownership and control over the public-service solutions they need. In short it means co-production.

Such a reorientation in the way that public services are routinely produced will involve moving away from providing centrally designed and controlled services – to citizens themselves designing and monitoring the delivery of the public services they require to achieve the most positive outcomes in their own lives. This is the essence of the co-production or active-partnership approach required if we are to have services oriented around delivering positive outcomes in people's lives - rather than public services that sometimes seem more concerned to meet the needs of various interest groups and the requirements of centralised bureaucracy.

Achieving such a change won't be easy. Quite apart from the process of identifying how to change the way we want to do things – itself a very big challenge – there will be the implementation challenge. This is where Ireland has historically failed over recent years – many argue that there is no shortage of good quality reform-oriented plans and strategies already in existence, but they have all suffered the same fate: implementation-failure.

We need to recognise that there will likely be high levels of cultural resistance in all institutions (including organisations in the community and voluntary sector) that have an interest, conscious or not, in maintaining the status quo.

All of that said, we can make a start by identifying the big themes that will drive change.

1. Agree the vision

Firstly, we need to agree that developing people's capabilities is indeed the objective of the society that we want to create. Everything else flows from that, so if we can't agree that then it will be very difficult to change the nature of our public services.

Good work was done in developing the high level goals in the Towards 2016 national agreement and these goals remain valid and should be re-subscribed to as a starting point to develop a renewed long term vision for national development. Useful work is also being done by the *Claiming our Future* movement, the *Citizens Assembly* and the *Conversation on Democracy* initiative which could also feed into developing such a national vision for change.

Why develop people's capabilities?

Because we have needs...
There is a grand context here: each of us are individual and unique members of humankind, a species-of-the-world that has been on a long evolutionary journey over hundreds of thousands of years from a constant struggle to secure the basic-necessities-of-being to one that has developed today the capabilities and technologies required to supply all the material goods and deliver the self-actualisation-potential of all people. Yet much of humanity still lives in poverty.

The basic necessities of being are the basic needs which we share as human beings: needs for shelter, food, clothing, belonging, and self-actualisation. We sometimes call these needs the human rights required to live life with dignity.

We are born into a world to which each of us has the same claim to belong, and from which each of us has the same claim to have the necessities of being, or our human needs met. This is a simple, but often forgotten fact.

None of us enter the world by an act of will or choice. None of us can be held individually responsible for the fact of our being or for the needs we experience as a result of our being: so why should we be held individually responsible for meeting these needs? Yet many societies, including our own, increasingly place responsibility on individuals to meet their needs for themselves.

While we experience the world as individuals, our very identities are not willed or chosen, but generated through the dynamic interaction between ourselves and the communities of which we are a part.

In a most profound way, we belong to one another, and we have a responsibility and a duty to ensure each other's needs are met.

...and because we have potential

Most of us have of a sense of our unrealised potential. We are aware of what we could have achieved for ourselves and others and could yet achieve for ourselves and others if we set our minds to it.

We are aware of the gap between who we are now and the person we could become, and have within us the potential to become. We are aware of the potential for our latent capabilities to be realised, and the corollary potential to stagnate or, worse, to be reduced or diminished. All of these are potentials.

We are also aware of the limitations, restrictions, and obstacles both within us, and in our circumstances and environment, that impede us - and the ones we love - from realising our capabilities and achieving our full developmental potential. Most of us shape our personal futures to some extent by imagining and envisioning what's possible, and then working – always reliant on others and operating within a broad social context - to achieve it.

Some of us are undoubtedly better than others at imagining our potential – or what's possible for ourselves - and then setting goals to achieve it. And many of us are either significantly advantaged or disadvantaged in achieving our potential by our situation in the unequal world we live in.

Most people – including those living in relative prosperity and comfort - want a better future for themselves, their families, friends, neighbours, colleagues and fellow citizens: a future that is in some way an improvement on the present, in terms of the material comforts they benefit from, the personal fulfilment and well-being they experience, the quality of relationships they enjoy. While perhaps not considering it in these terms, people wish to achieve their potential and fully develop their capabilities. Aristotle said that people want to be happy, and they are happy when they have achieved what is to be a human being, realising their full potential along the way.

We could perhaps reasonably say that the future we collectively want is a happier one in a society concerned to support and sustain happy people who have fully developed their capabilities.

2. Nurture values of public service

Once we have agreed that our ultimate objective is to develop people's capabilities then we need to work out the strategy to do this: the what and the how. Before turning to the what, let's take a quick look at the how. I would suggest that the concept of trusteeship is key here. Sharing responsibility recognises that each of us as individuals - and the communities we are a part of - belong to each other and have mutual responsibilities and obligations. Neither exists, nor can they be understood, in isolation.

It's worth reflecting a little here on what responsibility means.

If we have responsibility for a person's well-being, we have a duty to ourselves, to the person we are responsible with-and-for, and to the people who have entrusted us with that responsibility, to work together *in* a common mission to identify and serve the person's needs, and to co-account for our actions in the doing of that. Responsibility is always with-and-on-behalf-of ourselves and others in the context of an agreed overall strategy (whether stated or un-stated).

A person with such responsibility can be thought of as a trustee or guardian and guardianship carries both honour (at having been held by others in the high esteem and trust required) and responsibility. The concept of trusteeship throws light on what sharing responsibility involves. Trustees are people who have accepted an invitation from a wider community to take responsibility for tending to something on behalf of that wider community and, in the spirit of maintaining that trust, to voluntarily account for the way in which they deliver on their responsibility to that wider community.

Public service is simply trusteeship by another name.

We need to identify and nurture values of public service to re-create a positive culture of public service and trusteeship amongst all those who deliver public services – both statutory and voluntary. Society has a great deal to learn from the trustees of our charities and from how they overcome the challenge of governing themselves for the benefit of others, and in particular, from the self-control and flexibility-to-innovate that they demonstrate when they do it well.

There is now an opportunity to promote and nurture a new sense of national trusteeship amongst all people in positions of public and private authority in all public and private institutions where governance lapses contributed to the demoralised position we find ourselves in.

3. Identify the positive outcomes we aim to deliver

Once we have agreed the vision, and re-committed to the values of public service and trusteeship that will underpin our approach to the work (the how), we will need to identify the what: the actual positive outcomes (the positive change in quality of life) we are aiming to achieve in people's lives through our public services.

We will also need to ensure that the public servants and trustees to whom we delegate authority to deliver these outcomes have the flexibility required to be innovative in identifying the most effective way of delivering these outcomes.

If devolution of the governance of the provision of public services to local communities and voluntary-led organisations is to take place confidently, people will need to be assured that scarce public resources are being applied to maximum effect. Community and voluntary organisations therefore need to demonstrate a strong focus on maximising the impact and outcomes of their work for the people they serve.

Social enterprises, charities and other voluntary organisations are facing many challenges in the current difficult economic climate having to provide for increased demand for services while incomes fall from statutory grants and public donations

While achieving a strategic focus on delivering (and measuring) positive impact and outcomes presents a big challenge for well-resourced public agencies and private for-profit companies, it presents an even bigger challenge for social enterprises and voluntary non-profits that focus all their scarce energies and resources on meeting clients' immediate needs. So we need to provide our charities and voluntary groups with dedicated supports and resources to assist them to focus on improving their practice in the area of measuring impact and outcomes.

Delivering outcomes is a big challenge – because the distinction between inputs, outputs and outcomes is poorly understood in both the public and community and voluntary sectors.

Too often we account for our activities by focussing on whether we produced the action or thing we agreed we would produce (an output), rather than focussing on whether that output produced the intended positive outcome in the quality of life of the person concerned. The challenge here is to focus on outcomes rather than outputs.

As public service providers, we need to be clear about the improvements we aim to bring about through our work in the lives of the people or groups we serve. To do this we need to structure and govern our activities around identifying and delivering the actual improvement (the outcome) that people themselves require. Once we are implementing a strategy rooted in delivering the improvement we are trying to bring about in people lives, we will need to know whether we are actually delivering these outcomes – and to do this we need to develop outcome-indicators that allow us to measure the improvement in the quality of life, or life experience that the service has brought about. This means putting the person at the heart of our public services and working with them to identify the most appropriate indicators and ensuring that they are central to the monitoring process to ensure these outcomes are being produced.

There is a great deal of work that needs to be done to raise awareness of, and apply the skills and measurement tools necessary, to enable service providers to focus on delivering and accounting for outcomes-achieved rather than outputs-produced.

The NESC has produced some path-finding work in the form of *The Wellbeing Report* which identifies some outcome-measures that could be used as a basis for re-setting outcome targets for service provision. Working groups established during the implementation of *Towards 2016* also developed a suite of indicators that could be promoted as a basis for organisational re-focussing on outcomes.

Adopting measuring techniques such as SROI (Social Return on Investment) may be appropriate for large service providers, but the real challenge is to raise awareness of the many useful and appropriate tools and techniques that exist to enable all organisations, no matter how small, to measure the quality of their service and set outcome indicators and gauge progress in achieving them.

There is also much that can be learned from the private sector's application of the marketing approach which puts the identification and satisfaction of a customer's needs at the centre of the manufacturing and service-provision process.

I am not suggesting the wholesale application of the marketing approach to the delivery of public services, but when private firms do it well, when they take the time to focus on providing the customer with the experience they require, it is beyond argument that everyone benefits, customers and producers alike. Focussing on the experience is focussing on the outcome. There is learning here for all public service providers.

The marketing approach also positions the service provider as exactly that, a provider of service. Provided by a servant, maybe even a public servant. In our port-modern age we have become uncomfortable with the idea of servants, and perhaps with the very idea of service itself.

One of the challenges we face is returning dignity to the idea of service: where service is respected as a manifestation of care, and not viewed as self-serving, false and cynical at one extreme, or servile and weak at the other. Indeed, it could be argued that we would all benefit from adopting an attitude of service towards each other at all times, and that it is this attitude of service that characterises the essence of trusteeship and guardianship.

4. Create structures, systems and processes to co-produce these positive outcomes and return power to communities of place and interest

We have recognised that positive outcomes are co-produced in service user's lives by providers and service users working together. So the next challenge is to devise structures, systems and processes that put the service user at the centre of the design and monitoring process by providing either choice, or control, and ideally both. Current reforms in the approach to designing individualised social supports around people's needs in the area of disability services and home-care packages for elderly people demonstrate that putting the person at the heart of services is an achievable objective. We have noted the marketing approach in the private sector and the work we need to do to return dignity and respect to the ideas of service.

At the community level, involving people more thoroughly in the governance of their local communities should be aided through the local government reforms being advanced by government. Structures such as the County Development Boards, the Strategic Policy Committees and the Community Fora have underperformed in terms of involving local communities in policy making. These structures can undoubtedly be reformed and enhanced to better involve communities in community-level decision making. The *Conversation on Democracy/People* Talk initiative is, for example, proposing using innovative citizens' juries to facilitate communities to identify solution to their needs.

Census 2006 data produced by the CSO (2009) estimates that almost two-thirds (65%) of persons aged 16 and over participated in at least one community/voluntary group activity. Overall, nearly one-quarter (24%) of people participated in informal, unpaid charitable work. The most common form of group activity reported was religious (48%), followed by recreational (36%). This compares with just 4% reporting involvement in political groups (CSO, 2009). We can see the challenge: supporting people to get more involved in governing and shaping their communities at the traditionally understood "political" level.

While people and communities are clearly happy to participate in their community life, and do so in great numbers, they are not used to participating in decision-making of the political variety. Participating in this kind of decision-making can be thought of as active citizenship. Active Citizenship was flavour of the month a few years ago, and the challenge remains: what can we do to create conditions that support more active citizenship by people who want to get involved?

Voices from The Wheel's consultation on Active Citizenship, April 2006

"An active citizen is someone who exercises rights as well as responsibilities and is involved in community/local life in general, such as voting and using it wisely, taking part in neighbourhood watch schemes or youth work, being involved in local/ community politics. It is a democratic way of being that should be promoted."

"Active citizenship can only come about from people's confidence and faith that they will be heard"

"Being an active citizen means being involved in your community from the lowest level to the highest level. Building the capacity of your community, organising / taking part / representing / raising awareness of key issues / working towards the betterment of community and civil society."

5. Support community and voluntary organisations as facilitators of community involvement and active citizenship

Community and voluntary organisations play a vital part in the life of communities, enabling people to come together for their own purposes and take part in community activity by engaging in social or leisure pursuits, helping themselves and others, or promoting a cause they feel strongly about. Voluntary and community organisations are, as a result, very important facilitators of *community involvement.*

It is a truism that it is good for society that communities be able to organise; but it is also true that some communities are better able to organise than others. There are different levels of organisational capacity in diverse communities ranging from well-connected and resourced voluntary groups in well-off urban areas to poorly resourced community groups in disadvantaged urban or rural communities, and no groups at all in areas surrounding fragmented, or ghost, housing estates.

There is a risk that unless organisational capacity is provided for all areas of society, active-citizenship will become the preserve of well-organised, relatively well-off, sections of society, ironically increasing the risk of social exclusion faced by disadvantaged people and communities.

Achieving social inclusion depends on our commitment to ensure that active citizenship embraces principles of community development. This approach will allow people to have, as of right, the opportunity to influence and participate in the decisions that affect them. Supporting the capacity to organise, especially in disadvantaged communities, will also have the effect of improving the level of engagement with the political process at local level thereby reducing alienation and strengthening democracy.

We need to unambiguously recognize that
"An active community and voluntary sector contributes to a democratic, pluralist society, provides opportunities for the development of decentralised and participative structures and fosters a climate in which the quality of life can be enhanced for all".[54]

Community and voluntary organisations:

- provide a wide range of opportunities for active citizenship to express itself: both the issues they address and their aims and objectives act as a powerful catalyst to engagement by citizens
- provide a platform for individuals - including those who are marginalised - to voice their concerns and challenge government actions and policies
- bring people together and build social capital, facilitating collective action
- transmit and develop the values that underpin democracy (such as dialogue and respect) and familiarise people with democratic processes
- provide a good entry point to active citizenship: positive experiences of involvement in the sector provide a taste for involvement and can lead to further involvement

Any attempt at creating an environment that supports and encourages people to become active citizens will involve:

- volunteer groups being listened to; empowering people; involving people in decision-making and ensuring the views of citizens are taken on board by politicians and public authorities, enabling participation

---

[54] White Paper, Supporting Voluntary Activity, para 1.4, page 4

- support for participation by those most disadvantaged and without voice
- women, children and young people being involved in decision-making
- financial support from government for voluntary organisations and for community development activity
- Resources for people to participate in volunteer work; providing and promoting services and supports for volunteers and volunteer-involving organisations so that people know where to start if they want to participate in their communities
- active citizens not being seen by elected representatives or public servants as a nuisance, but as an asset
- reflecting on what it is to be a citizen in the state and on what type of society we would like to actively participate in, reflections in the form of a national dialogue on citizenship and an ongoing dialogue between the community and voluntary sector and the state.

So, communities need supports in the areas of supporting volunteering and active citizenship in all its forms.

The crisis in the public finances has placed tremendous strains on all charities with many seeing 20% to 25% plus drops in their income since 2008. Supporting charities and community and voluntary organisations to innovate in generating sustainable income sources (through for example making use of sources of social finance) has never been more important. The Wheel has made a series of recommendations for a thriving community and voluntary sector. I include these recommendations here.

The Wheel's recommendations for a thriving community and voluntary sector.

Why care about our community and voluntary sector?
Every year over two-thirds of Irish adults – that's over two million people - participate in the myriad of social, sporting, cultural and humanitarian activities offered by our 19,000 community and voluntary organisations. Community and voluntary organisations

employed over 40,000 full-time and 23,000 part-time staff in 20043 - with volunteers providing the equivalent full-time work of a further 31,000 people.

We need a coherent policy framework and a national development strategy for the community and voluntary sector. Our charities and community and voluntary organisations work constantly to improve their effectiveness in supporting the communities we serve – but this work is hampered by the fragmented nature of government policy towards the sector.

Government should take the lead and provide a coherent policy framework - including a national development strategy - for the sector. We also need to make sure that spaces for dialogue are available for discussions on sector-development issues between the sector and the State.

- Government should work with our sector to deliver a nationwide support-infrastructure so that our community and voluntary organisations receive the services and supports that are needed.
- We need a new framework for partnership working between the sector and the state, one that deepens the existing social partnership approach. Many charities and community and voluntary organisations work in partnership with Government bodies to provide essential services and supports for our people. Partnership working is complex and demanding, requiring strong shared understandings by both voluntary and statutory partners if beneficial outcomes are to be maximised for the people and communities we serve. We need a new framework for partnership working that sets out:
  – the principles that would inform the partnership-engagement when community and voluntary organisations work with statutory agencies
  – a mechanism to develop, drive implementation, and monitor/review a new agreement

- a new statutory funding regime that makes provision for multi-annual funding.
- Funding that is provided on a full-cost-recovery basis and
- Funding that includes training and pension budgets for staff.
• We need to simultaneously develop a strategy to diversify funding for the sector. Over 60% of funding for our community and voluntary organisations comes from the state – the sector needs to develop a strategy to diversify this funding mix in the context of the crisis in the public finances
• Government should involve our communities in designing our public services. Our community and voluntary organisations provide good locations for government to involve people in designing more responsive public services
• We need to make sure that the Charities Act 2009 provides supportive regulation for the community and voluntary sector, and that charities are resourced appropriately to respond to the challenges regulation will pose.
• The right of charities to engage in advocacy activity must be protected.
• Government should encourage volunteering and support voluntary trustees in their work by continuing to develop a national policy on volunteering
• Government should incentivise private-giving through extending tax relief on donations
• Government should introduce a VAT refund scheme for charities so that charities can spend all the money they get from donors on beneficiaries

6. Resource communities adequately from public funds

It is widely acknowledged that Ireland's tax take is amongst the lowest in the EU. We cannot provide the social, health and welfare services we require for ourselves and our families, friends, neighbours and fellow citizens if we continue to under-tax ourselves, forcing people to secure what should be public services privately or to go without and endure the resulting poverty.

Ireland can and should increase its tax take to 35%of GDP (from the less than 30% it is now) to ensure that we have the public resources required to deliver outcomes in the way we have been describing. Despite all the negative economic developments in recent years, Ireland remains a wealthy country. We must make sure that private resources that are under-taxed, or not taxed at all, are brought into the tax net and that everyone makes their fair contribution to providing the public resources required.

We labour under an illusion that we are a highly taxed country: we need to acknowledge that we are not, and begin to have a mature debate about the tax-take we need to support the society that we want, and stop the interminable discussion about what we can afford. Affordability comes into play of course, but it should only come into play when we have worked out what we want, and have moved on to thinking about what our priorities should be as we work towards delivering that vision for ourselves. Instead, we seem to dispense with the vision and spend all our energies fighting over what we can afford when we don't know what we want to buy.

We must facilitate local provision by resourcing communities adequately (from public funds raised through the taxation system) and enabling local communities to link with communities nationwide and internationally to identify solutions that would be better delivered regionally, nationally or indeed internationally.

A move to universal health insurance (paid by the state for those who require support) is the single most significant initiative that could be undertaken to ensure adequate resourcing of health and social services for people – and it is essential if the necessary funds are to be available to reform health and social service provision around individual needs.

7. Support those we delegate to deliver these outcomes on our behalf

To do all of this we need to change the way that public servants and trustees in community and voluntary, public-benefit organisations are held to account. We need to move from the current risk-averse system that rewards accounting for inputs expended, to one that rewards calculated risk-taking and innovation to deliver positive outcomes in people's lives.

We often associate responsibility with absolutes. We hear about people who are responsible for things having *to* carry the can if it goes wrong. We hear that we need invasive scrutiny (like some particularly gruesome radical surgery) of those responsible for delivering public services and that they should face gaol if they fail to discharge their responsibility (like explosives).

We hear that we need complete transparency and absolute accountability from those responsible to us. It can sometimes seem that people who accept responsibility must prepare to be pilloried and put on the rack if they fail. Is it any wonder people shrink from positions of public responsibility? Where is the room in this model for learning from mistakes? For innovation to take place people must be free to take calculated risks.

While there is no doubt that there have been profound governance failures over the years that contributed to causing our social and economic crisis, while there are indeed people who engaged in criminal behaviour and while governance practice can undoubtedly be improved in almost every area of public and private life, I suggest the blaming everything on the failures of an irresponsible and unaccountable few misses the point.

The real issue is that we as a people have delegated more and more authority for public decision making to elected representatives and public servants without investing in the reporting-back systems that make responsible delegation possible in any other walk of life. It can be argued that our system allows us to place all responsibility for meeting (and blame for not meeting) our public-service needs on our elected representatives and on public servants because there is currently nowhere else to place that responsibility.

Our elected representatives report back once every five years at a general election. This is wholly inadequate in the context of the modern developmental welfare state we aspire to become. This democratic deficit lies at the heart of the governance failures we have experienced and explains in part the backlash against those perceived to have been responsible for failing in their responsibilities. Oireachtas reform, electoral reform, and reform in the way Government appointments are made are all key, but beyond the scope of consideration here.

In the meantime, co-producing public services aimed at developing people's capabilities, and returning real authority and power to local communities, will enable people to play the vital role of holding elected representatives, public servants and trustees directly accountable on an ongoing basis. It will also allow people to share in responsibility with elected representatives and public servants for ensuring positive outcomes, and make it clear that we all should be (and already are) sharing some responsibility in and for the public services available to us.

Rising to the Challenge

This would be a truly bottom-up approach that puts people at the heart of public services. We have an opportunity now to ensure that the public services reform process results in improved outcomes for all users of public services - and that's all of us. Can we achieve the changes we seek?

Can we have strong communities where people lead fulfilled lives, with a sense of both authority over, and responsibility for meeting, their community and individual needs, using public resources made available as a right for that purpose?

Can we do this and still benefit from people who feel encouraged to innovate and who can privately benefit from the entrepreneurialism that drives so much good in human progress to date? I believe we can.

Where to start? What to do?

What are the implications of the concept of sharing responsibility if we are to move in the direction indicated? Many challenges will accompany this new approach, including:

1. Providing the resources – raising sufficient taxation

We have to recognise that we have a duty to raise sufficient taxation to pay for the public services that people have a right to expect. Taxation approaches based on beggar-thy-neighbour-tax-policies merely seek to reinforce the current, failed economic development model and will condemn us to repeating the failures of the past, even if we somehow manage to buy our way out of the current crisis (at a completely unacceptable price).

We have to re-forge the relationship in people's minds to taxation being one of the primary ways in which we express social solidarity by funding the services we all require to deliver the outcomes everyone has a right to expect.

2. Encouraging participation

Many people have become used to non-participation in organising and governing community services. If people had a meaningful opportunity to participate in designing and monitoring the delivery of health, social and community services then they would see what is being done with the available public monies, understand the services they are entitled to, and participate in reaching shared understandings about what services should be available where, thus avoiding the unproductive reverse-nimbyism that understandably accompanies current centralised announcements regarding changes – invariably cuts - in levels of local service provision.

There are many practical things we can do to support the participation of volunteers in national life

- Continue to develop a national policy on volunteering.
- Continue the roll out of a comprehensive, national services and supports infrastructure at local level for people who are looking to volunteer by building on the nation volunteers' centres network.
- Address the way in which the tax and benefit systems interact to create income-traps and disincentives for people who might have the time to volunteer
- Develop solutions to enable time-poor people to participate in their communities
- Ensure that the level of resources being provided to communities (whether advice/training, public funding or tax relief on private donations) takes account of the varying levels of need in different communities, so that there are genuinely equal opportunities for all to volunteer and make a difference in their own community.
- Volunteers and active citizens play an important role as agents-of-change and this inevitably involves them in challenging established ways of doing things. We must ensure that there is a change in the mindset at all levels of state bureaucracy so that people who participate are not seen as a nuisance but as essential participants if our society is to be inclusive of active citizens. It's that point about service again.

With regard to formal participation in electoral processes and local democratic structures, there is a widely shared sense of concern about the declining numbers participating in democratic processes. But again, there are practical things we can do in this area

- Charge an independent *Electoral Commission* with promoting electoral participation generally and making funding available to organisations to deliver programmes to increase voter participation - particularly participation by disadvantaged people.
- Develop citizenship education at all levels of the education system.
- Establish and resource a forum for dialogue on civil society issues – building on and taking into account the work of initiatives such as *Claiming our Future*, the *We The Citizens*, the *Conversation on Democracy/People Talk* project and the *Community and Voluntary Pillar*.

- Support and resource more participative structures and processes at local level (such as the *citizens juries* approach) that put people at the heart of local planning

3. Providing incomes sufficient to live life with dignity

We have already noted that people have a legitimate expectation, a right, call it what you will, to be cared for as human beings by the human society they are part of. When considered deeply, there are truly profound implications that flow from recognising this fact.

Recognition means no longer accepting that if a person does not, or cannot, earn a living (as traditionally understood through doing a paid job) then they either live in poverty or become dependent on the charity of others (or on means tested benefits). People have a right to live with dignity, and to enjoy a standard of living acceptable to all.

True shared social responsibility recognises that societies should support and maximise the autonomy of people by ensuring that everyone receives an unconditional guaranteed basic income (without any means test or work requirement) that is sufficient for them to live a life with dignity. All income earned above this level of guaranteed basic income could be taxed. To many, the idea will seem revolutionary – but it's only a logical extension of accepting the principle that everyone has a right to live autonomously, with dignity and respect.

A range of studies (including a Green Paper[55]) have shown that a basic income system could be introduced in Ireland and could be paid for while maintaining a competitive economy and protecting social services.

4. Good governance: supporting trusteeship

Governance is the art of organisational self-control and direction-setting, and when we are controlling things that do not belong to us (such as our public institutions, large private, quoted firms - such as banks - and our voluntary and community organisations) we have an extra special duty to

---

[55] Department of the Taoiseach (2002), *Basic Income: A Green Paper*, Dublin: Department of the Taoiseach

make sure we are applying the highest possible standards on behalf of the people who have entrusted it to our custodianship.

Clearly, delegating authority to communities and service users to put them in control of community, social and health services will involve local groups and organisations – governed by trustees – assuming a more central role in our public affairs. We need to develop a fuller appreciation of the unique position of trustees in the organisation of our collective affairs – people who have quasi-private responsibility for public assets.

Ensuring that all community organisations are governed well, are transparent in their decision-making and that they are accountable to their local communities will therefore be very important. We cannot afford to replace unaccountable, centralised state bureaucracies, which can in theory be held accountable by elected representatives, with unaccountable voluntary trustees.

We will need to maintain an intense focus on good governance practice in community and voluntary organisations. This can partly be accomplished by the pending Charities Regulatory Authority, but it will in much larger part be accomplished by encouraging and supporting voluntary organisations to adopt best governance practice in the management of the public resources entrusted to them.

The Wheel is working with colleagues in a consortium of leaders in the community and voluntary sector to develop a *Code of Governance* for voluntary organisations in Ireland. When launched it is proposed that all charities and community and voluntary organisations adopt this code. It could be proposed that all charities report on their adherence to the code (on a comply or explain basis) in the annual reports they will be required to submit to the Charities Regulator on full commencement of the Charities Act 2009.

Additionally, it is clear that ongoing support from public funding sources will be required to support a continuing focus on the good governance of charities, and it will be crucial that infrastructural supports to support the good governance of charities continue to be available - funded from the public purse - in the years ahead.

5. Frameworks for co-production and partnership

Many community and voluntary organisations are involved in delivering publicly funded services. They often help public service commissioners to identify and understand people's needs, and at the same time enable users to have a real say in the services delivered. It is argued, however, that moves to contracts and service agreements between public funders and voluntary service-deliverers have squeezed out the full value that voluntary organisations provide.

Evidence suggests that while contracting arrangements and performance management systems have caused some voluntary and community organisations to become more professional, they have also become more bureaucratic as a consequence.

Certain positive characteristics are routinely associated with the voluntary, non-profit approach to meeting social need - characteristics that undoubtedly lead to improved outcomes for the people served. These include:

- services tailored to individual need through a person-centred approach
- innovation in service design, delivery and funding
- flexibility
- rapidity in responding to new and emergent need
- a value-for-money focus (driven by a constant need to manage scare resources in the face of unmet need)
- involvement of users/beneficiaries in design and control
- commitment of value-driven personnel who choose to work in the sector
- empowerment (and associated well-being benefits) of people and communities involved
- high quality strategic leadership and governance provided by volunteer trustees motivated solely to deliver the highest quality outcomes to meet people's needs

If community and voluntary organisations are to preserve these positive characteristics of their approach to their work, engage productively with their statutory counterparts, and maintain the required focus on delivering the best possible outcomes in services-users lives, then high levels of mutual trust and shared understandings of the task at hand will be required.

We need to ensure that a culture of contactarianism does not come to dominate this special public-benefit space. To avoid this, we need to develop, formally adopt, and apply and implement clear frameworks and codes for partnership working to guide collaborative working by public-sector and voluntary/not-for-profit organisations when working together to deliver public-benefit outcomes.

The Wheel has worked over the last few years to develop a *New Framework for Partnership Working* - to build on the approach identified in the *White Paper Supporting Voluntary Activity* – to govern and inform working relationships between statutory agencies and voluntary organisations in Ireland.

At The Wheel's May 2011 conference, Minister Phil Hogan noted "I am prepared to continue the *structured dialogue process* with the members of the Community & Voluntary Pillar that was announced by the previous Government earlier this year". That structured dialogue process committed government *"to engage with the Community and Voluntary Pillar on how to progress development of future frameworks to support the deepening of the partnership between statutory bodies and voluntary and community organisations"* and proposed the following approach:

Structured Dialogue with the Community & Voluntary Pillar.

A set of principles would underpin the deepening of the relationship and inform engagements between officials and stakeholders. A number of the joint principles set out in the White Paper are particularly relevant in this context:

I. Both Sectors value openness, accountability and transparency in the relationships between the State and the Community and Voluntary sector.

II. There is a shared commitment by both the State and the Sector to ensure the involvement of consumers and people who avail of services in the planning, delivery, management and evaluation of policy and programmes. This applies at all levels: national, regional and local.

III. There is a joint commitment relating to fostering co-operation and the co-ordination within and across each Sector as well as between the State and the Community and Voluntary Sector.

IV. There is a commitment on the part of both the State and the sector to provide access to, and to share, information relevant to the pursuit of shared objectives.

V. The State and the sector commit themselves to carrying out periodic and mutually agreed monitoring and evaluation of their individual actions, as well as joint evaluation of the experience of operating this framework.

VI. The State and the sector each recognise their respective rights and shared objective in relation to developing and implementing effective policy, including the right to constructively critique each other's actions and policies, in a context of mutual respect.

VII. There is a commitment to developing mutual understanding of the culture and operating principles of each Sector and to take practical steps to achieve this.

VIII. Both Sectors commit themselves to using working methods that are flexible and efficient in the context of the growing demands and range of tasks posed by modern society.

Elements for a Bilateral Engagement

Engagements between the Department of Community, Equality & Gaeltacht Affairs and the C&V Pillar to be mutually beneficial and solutions focused. Meetings to have a consistent format, with a sharply focused agenda, which is agreed and balanced for each side. Meetings would be focused on:

- outline plans, strategies, legislation
- information about developments
- possible mutual approaches to addressing challenges
- feedback on how actions are impacting and practical suggestions for resolving any unintended effects
- feedback on suggestions or ideas
- opportunities for improved information, integration, efficiency, etc.
- strengthening relationships

This commitment to structured dialogue from the new government is encouraging and could, if implemented (the old implementation challenge again) set a positive example for a new model for public-benefit, partnership working in the years ahead.

6. Encourage Advocacy

Critical to any partnership where public funding and resource allocation is under the control of elected representatives is of course power and how it is applied and regulated. In the new dispensation we are exploring, it will be vital to ensure that advocacy by community groups and organisations is seen as a necessary part of the policy-formation process leading to better outcomes, and that it is supported and encouraged by all public authorities, with advocating organisations and communities accepting that there are responsibilities that go with effective advocacy.

The *Advocacy Initiative* is a consortium of Irish community and voluntary organisations that have come together to explore the development (amongst many other advocacy related considerations) of a Code of Good Advocacy practice to enable voluntary organisations to regulate their own advocacy practice against benchmarks and standards of advocacy practice developed by the sector for itself.

Conclusion: a vision to inspire

We are all sharing responsibility in shaping the future whether we are aware of it or not. There are lots of things we can do (some of which we have identified here) to ensure that this process is more consciously structured and directed to improve the lives of all our people, of all the people on our finite planet and the future of our life-giving planet itself.

So let's finish with what's possible, on an inspiring note, a vision it seems reasonable to strive for.

An Ireland where individuals and their families, friends, communities, and neighbours share responsibility with government, the public and private sectors, community and voluntary organisations and civil society in a co-endeavour to realise everyone's capabilities and developmental potential.

Our new Ireland would be characterised by:

- A sense of national mission towards delivering our shared vision of the society we want for our family, friends, neighbours, fellow citizens, and people of the world
- everyone receives a basic income sufficient to live life with dignity and no one lives in poverty
- equal dignity attaches to all work and people are valued for the non-commercial caring and nurturing work they do in the home
- People derive primary satisfaction from the contribution they make to their communities rather than from the money they earn and things they can buy
- service is respected as a manifestation of a caring attitude, and not viewed as false and insincere or servile and weak
- the honour – and the responsibility - in public service being recognised
- People are encouraged to explore their aptitudes and capabilities and make work and career choices on the basis of those aptitudes and capabilities
- People give as much time and resources as they can to other people and to their communities
- People are happy to be actively involved in the governance of their local communities and their public services (a function that in longer "hived off" to professional representatives)

- social entrepreneurship becoming the norm for all entrepreneurship; the purpose of entrepreneurialism being the experience of satisfaction at having delivered positive outcomes for society, rather than to personally enrich the entrepreneur (which is a by-product of successful entrepreneurialism)
- Public services are designed around people's needs (person centeredness underpinned by an attitude of service and mutual respect)
- Economic paradigm shifts from profit-seeking perpetual growth (and recession) to developing people's capabilities in a sustainable way
- Invention and innovation continue to play a central role in human development – as a result the true motive to invent and innovate: to provide a solution people will benefit from to a shared challenge people face.
- People are rewarded for the fruits of their labour – and where people can expect to personally benefit from their entrepreneurial activity – but in a context where the level of personal benefits bears reasonable relation to equity for the community at large.
- Where the environment is seen as our nurturer, to be minded and protected from exploitation.

8.
Sharing Responsibility for Shaping the Future - Why and How?

Seán Healy and Brigid Reynolds

Introduction

In recent decades intellectual and political elites have paid little attention to issues concerning the future. Those who raised questions concerning the future, what it might look like, how it should be shaped and who should play a part in deciding its shape were dismissed as being out of touch with the 'real' world. It was regularly pointed out to such questioners that the market would make these decisions and there wasn't much point in wasting time 'theorising' about such issues. Media coverage of events and discussions concerning issues rarely focused on the future and what its shape might be. The so-called 'experts' who were consulted, who appeared on TV and radio programmes and wrote extensively in newspapers were mostly economists. It seemed that everything could be reduced to its economic dimensions and only economists had a useful contribution to make to the discussion and problem-solving. The crises of recent years have highlighted the paucity of this approach.

Since 2007 the world's economy has been in turmoil. The world's political structures have failed to deal with this turmoil in a fair and just manner. Yet the failure for the most part to address the future in anything more than economic and fiscal terms displays a profound lack of awareness of the issues at stake. Of course the economic issues are very important but so are the political, the cultural, the social and the environmental. There is an urgent need for discussion of the vision of the future that is guiding decision-making across the board. But to raise this issue leads very quickly to being dismissed in the media, and sometimes even by Government, as being out of touch with the 'real' world. Such dismissal comes from people and institutions whose world seems confined to economic and fiscal issues only. These are important issues but they are far from being the whole story. By contrast, there has been a sea-change for the general public although it should be noted in passing that this change has not manifested itself in much of the media's coverage of events or discussion of issues, including the future.

Ireland has been hit by five interlinked crises i.e. banking, public finances, economic, social and reputational[56] (NESC 2009). Many people have seen the multi-layered series of crises that have hit the world's economy and political structures and come to the conclusion that the basic model underpinning the world's development is broken, perhaps irreparably. Others argue that this conclusion is unfair and believe that slight adjustments are all that are required to rectify the problems currently being encountered. Either way, there is a growing clamour concerning the future, what it should be like and who should shape it; people are demanding that their voices be heard when decisions, especially those concerning the future, are being made. They have lost their belief in the market as the ultimate decider and they have little or no confidence in the current political structures, nationally or internationally, having the capacity to address these issues. They see much of what has been done in the past four years as incompetent at best.

In Ireland's case there is much agreement that the decisions taken in the period since 2007 have been unfair and unjust. Many would agree that:

- While Ireland meets the various benchmarks contained in the Bailout Agreement it has with the International Monetary Fund, the European Central Bank and the European Commission, the bailout framework conditions and benchmarks are producing a process of dispossession of those who are poor and/or vulnerable.
- Those being dispossessed by this Agreement had no hand, act or part in making the decisions that caused the problems in the first place.

---

[56] For a detailed outline of these crises cf. National Economic and Social Council (2009), *Ireland's Five Part Crisis*, Dublin, NESC.

- The 'gambling bankers' and their like are having all their losses repaid by the Irish tax-payer even though they knowingly undertook the risks involved in their original gamble.
- The Agreement itself is leading to profits of €9bn for the EU segment alone of the Troika.
- This process is failing to address the situation of moral hazard in which banks and financial institutions in the EU and beyond are protected from the consequences of their actions while innocent poor and vulnerable people are dispossessed,
- The European Central Bank and the European Commission both played a role in the decisions that caused Ireland's problems. Now, however, these institutions refuse to accept their share of responsibility. Instead, they insist that people who played no role in these decisions (i.e. Ireland's poor and vulnerable) must pay in full to reimburse these institutions.
- This is a profoundly immoral process.
- Much of what has been done at 'official' level to address the current series of crises has seriously damaged the well-being of a great many people.

Given this situation major questions arise concerning the future and how it is to be shaped. Among the most important questions to which answers are required are:

- Why should responsibility be shared?
- How can responsibility be shared in a real and meaningful manner at local, national and international levels?
- How can people ensure their voice is really heard or that future generation, and the environment, are protected?

This chapter seeks to provide some responses to these questions.

1. Why?

There are many reasons why responsibility for shaping the future should be shared. Here we identify six and elaborate a little on each. We will then move on to address the question how? The six reasons we focus on are:

- To ensure priority is given to well-being and the Common Good
- To deal with the challenges of markets and their failures
- To address other challenges in a manner most likely to succeed
- To link rights and responsibilities
- To work towards a new paradigm more appropriate for the 21st century
- To protect the interests of future generations.

1.1 To ensure priority is given to well-being and the Common Good

1.1.1 Well-being

In recent years there have been many useful discussions and publications on the issue of well-being. The National Economic and Social Council (NESC) defined well-being as follows: "A person's well-being relates to their physical, social and mental state. It requires that basic needs are met, that people have a sense of purpose, and that they feel able to achieve important goals, to participate in society and to live the lives they value and have reason to value." (NESC 2009, p.xiii) This is the well-being that *Social Justice Ireland* and the present authors would like for all members of all societies.

As far back as Plato it was recognised that the person grows and develops in the context of society. "Society originates because the individual is not self-sufficient, but has many needs which he can't supply himself"[57]. The person grows and develops through relationships with people; family, neighbours, community, wider society. Down through the ages various philosophies and social arrangements have been proposed to meet the felt need in societies to fulfil their perceived obligations to their members. These varied from Aristotle's position of favouring private ownership but common use of property to ensure the dire needs of people were met, to

---
[57] (Plato, in Lee 1987, p58, cited in George, V. 2010, p6)

the emphasis of both Plato and Aristotle that education should be free and compulsory, to Cicero's discussion of equality, to the early Christian emphasis on sharing and forming community.[58]

In more recent times the dignity of the person has been enshrined in The Universal Declaration of Human Rights which states: "All human beings are born free and equal in dignity and rights. They are endowed with reason and conscience and should act towards one another in a spirit of brotherhood." This core value is also at the heart of the Catholic Social Thought tradition. *Social Justice Ireland* and the authors in particular, support the values of both these traditions. We advocate that the dignity of each and every person must be recognised, acknowledged and promoted effectively. This implies that society's structures, institutions and laws should exist for the authentic development of the person.

1.1.2 The Common Good
The right of the individual to freedom and personal development is limited by the rights of other people. This leads to a second core value, namely, the common good. As we noted earlier the concept of the 'common good' originated over two thousand years ago in the writings of Plato, Aristotle and Cicero. More recently, the philosopher John Rawls defined the common good as "certain general conditions that are…equally to everyone's advantage" (Rawls, 1971 p.246). François Flahault notes "that the human state of nature is the social state, that there has never been a human being who was not embedded, as it were, in a multiplicity. This necessarily means that relational well-being is the primary form of common good. Just as air is the vital element for the survival of our bodies, coexistence is the element necessary for our existence as persons. The common good is the sum of all that which supports coexistence, and consequently the very existence of individuals." (Flahault, François, 2011: 68)

---

[58] For an interesting review of the historical development of welfare see George, V. (2010), *Major Thinkers in Welfare: Contemporary Issues in Historical Perspective*, Bristol, The Policy Press.

Social Justice Ireland understands the term 'common good' as "the sum of those conditions of social life by which individuals, families and groups can achieve their own fulfilment in a relatively thorough and ready way" (Gaudium et Spes 1965:74). This understanding recognises the fact that the person develops their potential in the context of society where the needs and rights of all members and groups are respected. The common good, then, consists primarily of having the social systems, institutions and environments on which we all depend, work in a manner that benefits all people simultaneously and in solidarity. The NESC study referred to already states that "at a societal level, a belief in a 'common good' has been shown to contribute to the overall well-being of society. This requires a level of recognition of rights and responsibilities, empathy with others and values of citizenship" (NESC, 2009, p.32).

This raises the issue of resources. The goods of the planet are for the use of all people – not just the present generation; they are also for the use of generations still to come. The present generation must recognise it has a responsibility to ensure that it does not damage but rather enhances the goods of the planet that it hands on – be they economic, cultural, social or environmental. The structural arrangements regarding the ownership, use, accumulation and distribution of goods are disputed areas. However it must be recognised that these arrangements have a major impact on how society is shaped and how it supports the well-being of each of its members in solidarity with others.

1.1.3 Responsibility and the Common Good

This discussion leads to the questions 'who is responsible for producing and protecting common goods and what do we mean by responsibility? Lorenzo Sacconi defines responsibility as follows: "being responsible means having the capacity to be subjected to blame or praise due to an action or the outcome of an action in terms of some norm (legal or moral) from which a duty is derived". He goes on to raise the question of what it means to have "the capability for being subjected to blame or praise." He answers the question with the postulate "ought implies can" so "one cannot be attributed responsibility for an act if one cannot make a choice regarding that action. This is rather obvious, but nonetheless it immediately raises a basic challenge to the definition of shared social responsibilities: we cannot share any responsibility with another (natural or legal) person if that person cannot make any choice in the matter." (Sacconi, 2011:30)

Claus Offe notes (Offe, 2011) that "arguably, there was a time when the question of 'who is responsible and therefore can be held accountable' was comparatively easy to answer." The answer was 'the incumbent government'. However it is more difficult to locate responsibility today. Offe points to four developments that have led to this difficulty.

a) Political elites have become "strategic agents that spend much of their time and resources on managing their mass constituency's *perception* of responsibility They do so in the three most common communicative modes by which elites address their constituencies: *blame avoidance* and finger-pointing (in the case of undesirable developments and outcomes), *credit claiming* (in the cases of favourable ones), and the rhetorical *taking* of (what they can safely assume on the basis of opinion polls) *popular positions*". These activities make it difficult to attribute responsibility for outcomes.

b) The opaqueness of the question of responsibility "has a foundation in changing institutional realities, having to do with the transformation of *government* into *governance*. While 'government' stands for the clearly demarcated and visible competency of particular governmental office-holders and parties in legislative chambers to make collectively binding decisions, 'governance' stands for more or less fleeting multi-actor alliances which span the divides between and private actors, state and civil society, or national and international actors." The more such alliances are formed the more difficult it is to link decisions with outcomes.

c) "...due to the endemic and seemingly chronic *fiscal crisis* that has befallen virtually every state in Europe (both as a consequence of them having transformed themselves into low-tax 'competition states' in an open global economy and as a consequence of the bailout-needs ensuing upon the financial market crisis), the range of matters that the state and political elites can at all credibly promise and take responsibility for, its very 'state capacity' has been shrinking quite dramatically."

d) "…fiscally starved governments have for several decades …resorted to strategies of shedding and re-assigning responsibilities. The basic intuition is that the government is not responsible, citizens themselves are 'responsibilised', with the only remaining role of government consisting in 'activating' and 'incentivising' citizens so that *they* live up to their *individual* responsibility rather than asking and expecting government to take responsibility *for* them."

Offe then goes on to examine the freedom of the individual to make choices. He notes the freely chosen action of individuals affect not just themselves, but others as well. "The freedom of choice of one person can be said to constrain the freedom of choice of others." Therefore in order for the "highest value of freedom to be universally enjoyed, it must be limited at the level of individuals through statutory regulation, rules of criminal law, etc."

Offe notes a second problem: the range of an individual's free choice is not just determined by legal guarantees securing it, but also by favourable or unfavourable *conditions* which can dramatically *expand* (e.g., through 'unearned' inherited wealth) or severely *restrict* (e.g., due to congenital physical handicaps or the fact of being born in a poor country) the range of choices individuals have at their disposal, particularly as these adverse conditions are due to 'brute luck' and can in no way be causally attributed to any behaviour that those benefitting or suffering from them are causally responsible for."

There has been little concern for the capability of citizens to make choices and cope with the outcomes. How do we relate capability to responsibility? There has been far too little discussion on how a level playing field can be put in place so that all people can interact effectively with the choices that confront them, share responsibility for the decisions taken and work towards desirable outcomes.

This issue was addressed by, among others, the Nobel prize-winning economist Amartya Sen. He criticises Rawls' theory of justice (Rawls, 1971) because he sees this theory as too linear in its understanding of how just situations can be achieved. He claims the assumption accepted by Rawls, that active and critical citizens with a keen interest in promoting justice will be able to influence institutional structures and that those structures will reflect citizens' concerns, is not enough. It does not recognise or realise that a mechanism is needed for an open political space in which a public debate about such contentious issues can be developed. Sen concludes that "to prevent catastrophes caused by human negligence or callous obduracy, we need critical scrutiny, not just goodwill towards others." (Sen, 2009: 48). Such critical, public scrutiny based on the human capacity to reason will be a key aspect in addressing the question of how to overcome inequality and injustice. "The role of unrestricted public reasoning is quite central to democratic politics in general and to the pursuit of social justice in particular". (Sen, 2009:44)

However, such public scrutiny requires a safe space or mechanism to enable an open and public dialogue on key issues and challenges.[59] For three decades Jurgen Habermas has argued for a free public sphere that would allow an unrestricted dialogue about the core values of a particular society. (Habermas, 2001) Fiedler summarises Habermas' view: "Such a dialogue should be maintained by a civil society that sets their own agendas and which is only regulated by the state insofar as the state ensures that the dialogue about value and belief systems happens in a democratic and domination-free setting." (Fiedler, 2011:10) We will return to the topic of civil society later in this paper. For now it is sufficient to note that the authors have argued for many years that such a public space is required and that civil society should play a key role in its establishment, development, action and evaluation. (Healy/Reynolds, 2000)

---

[59] These paragraphs draw extensively on an excellent paper by Dr Matthias Fiedler (Fiedler 2011) which sets out his thoughts on development as shared responsibility.

There is one final issue we wish to draw attention to before moving from this discussion on responsibility, well-being and the common good. Sen's views on 'capability' have been developed in some detail by the philosopher Martha Nussbaum. (Nussbaum, 2000) She has argued that there is a basic minimum threshold that everyone should meet and she argues that the most urgent challenge for all societies today is ensuring that no individual falls below this threshold. She identifies ten capabilities which all should have and claims a society is unjust if anyone does not have these. (Nussbaum 2000:78-80) We simply draw attention to this as one example of the importance of capability. If a person does not have the capability to attain basic well-being then that situation is unjust. Society and the state have a responsibility to do what is required to ensure this injustice is rectified. This responsibility is not confined to one's own country or society; it extends across the planet. Where well-being is concerned we are all our brothers' and sisters' keeper.

The common good has not received the attention it should receive in recent times. People's well-being has not been protected during recent crises. There has been much controversy and disagreement about who is or is not responsible for this. These critically important limitations must be addressed if there is to be a just and fair future. To address them effectively requires the development of new forms of dialogue that will renew people's confidence in the ability of public institutions (a) to maintain a focus on the common good and (b) to secure people's well-being. Later in this paper we will address the question of how this might be done. Here we continue our discussion on why responsibility in shaping the future must be shared.

1.2 To deal with the challenges of markets and their failures

Historically, the market was seen as a civilising mechanism[60]. For much of the eighteenth and early nineteenth centuries the generally accepted view

---

[60] For a detailed treatment of this and related issues cf. Hirschman, Hirschman AO, 1977, Rival interpretations of market society: civilizing, destructive or feeble? J. Con. Lit. 20: 1463-84; Marion Fourcade and Kieran Healy, *Moral Views of Market Society* in Annual Review of Sociology, 2007, 33, 285-311

was that markets made people friendlier and less inclined to fight one another. Marx, among others, rejected this view and believed that "capitalist society tends to undermine its own foundations, to the point at which it will ultimately self-destruct" (Fourcade/Healy, 2007:286). Those who believed in the market as a civilising influence revised their position to say that it was still performing this role, but in a rather feeble manner. This feebleness was attributed to cultural and institutional legacies from the past that made the market's exercise of its role more difficult. The United States of America was seen as having moral character and economic success because of the lack of such legacies. These understandings were summarised by Hirschman (1977) as markets being seen as civilising, destructive or feeble in their effects on society.

A great deal of the research in the decades following Hirschman's analysis fits within these three categories. Many economists are still arguing that the economy has a positive impact on civil society, politics and culture. This is the liberal understanding in today's world. It believes that greed will not gain the upper hand because an individual's greed will be kept in check by a similar greed in others, so self-interest will ensure that people will act in a polite and honest manner. According to this view in practice, commerce will promote cooperation. It is also seen as promoting freedom of the individual and of society. Likewise it is seen as promoting creativity and innovation.

Others are claiming that instead of cooperation the market produces coercion and exclusion. Sandel claims that severe inequality and/or dire economic necessity make a mockery of the formally free nature of market exchange (Sandel 2000). Some have concluded that "where the ideology of submission to the 'free market' has spread we observe a spectacular rise in the number of people being put behind bars as the state relies increasingly on policies and penal institutions to contain the social disorders produced by mass unemployment, the imposition of precarious wage work and the shrinking of social protection" (Wacquant 2001:404 cited in Fourcade/Healy 2007:293). Others claim that equating markets with democratic and personal freedom is simply a mechanism to provide legitimisation for free-market liberalism and is not based on objective analysis of the situation.

Others, again, believe that markets are embedded in, entangled with or otherwise dependent on other parts of society i.e. that they are not nearly as powerful, for good or ill, as some people claim (Beckert 2002).

Fourcade and Healy summarise today's version of Hirschman's three views as the liberal dream, the commodified nightmare and shackles/blessings. They go on to suggest a fourth dimension emerging in recent economic sociology literature which sees markets as moral projects. This understanding argues that markets are cultural because they are explicitly moral projects. They show this to be the case in three areas. Firstly, markets are seen as playing a role in establishing moral boundaries between persons or societies. For example, Max Weber in his classic study *The Protestant Ethic and the Spirit of Capitalism*, (1958) has shown that money is central to the evaluation of the moral worth of individuals. The careful management of one's wealth is not just economically rational but is a measure of one's moral responsibility.

Secondly, social scientists constantly comment on the moral dimensions of markets. Economists in particular are regularly called on, as the supposed experts, to play a leading role in the design of institutions whether these concern national development, corporate management or organisational reform. In this they are not just describing reality but actually shaping it for some purpose or other. This has profound moral implications. In Ireland the establishment of the Irish Fiscal Advisory Council, consisting of economists only, who will set the parameters for Government's Budgets, is an example of this in practice. Only economists are included in this body which will decide and advise on what is a profoundly moral project i.e. making recommendations that will shape the future of Ireland based on what they consider to be the good of Irish society.

Thirdly, Fourcade and Healy argue that economic exchange and policy making are saturated with moral statements (2007:303-4). They point out, for example, that issues such as transparency and corruption are used to monitor corporations, international institutions and countries. Understandings of what constitutes fair prices, fair wages, fair competition and fair trade are all based on moral views about what things are worth and what processes are just. What is most worrying in this context is that much of the rationalisation and moralising that takes place is dominated by economists and often is based on turning purely economic criteria such as efficiency or profit making into moral rules that must be followed.

It is clear that markets have failed dramatically on many occasions, most recently in the period following 2007. It is also clear that, following this most recent failure, political and economic institutions took action to protect market institutions such as banks. Governments and international bodies such as the IMF, the ECB and the European Commission made huge efforts and invested enormous resources in rescuing these banks which had gambled recklessly and lost their money. This was done at the expense of people who had played no part in causing the market's failure i.e. (a) taxpayers who had to pay through increased taxation and (b) all citizens, especially those who are poor or vulnerable, who paid through major reductions in services. A great many people were impacted on under both these headings. This was a process of systematic dispossession of those who were poor and/or vulnerable in which their resources were transferred to the banks and other market institutions through a series of political decisions. This process failed a great many people, especially those who were poor or marginalised. This process is deeply immoral. This is an example of where a few people made decisions but the burden of their decisions is forced on all members of society. In justice those who are expected to take responsibility for carrying the burden of decisions should have their voices and perspectives heard in making these decisions. It is one further reason why responsibility must be shared in the processes that shape the future.

1.3 To address other challenges in a manner most likely to succeed

Another reason responsibility needs to be shared in shaping the future flows from an analysis of how people tend to respond to great challenges or dangers. How people should respond was once a matter discussed in theology but today this issue arises widely as people face terror, pandemics, environmental devastation, nuclear annihilation, and many other threats to their very existence. The planet itself, or at least the people who inhabit it, are at risk. Freud argued that the standard psychological response to an overwhelming danger is denial. But, far more convincingly, sociologist Robert Wuthnow, has argued the opposite. (Wuthnow, 2010) In his book 'Be Very Afraid' he argues convincingly that we seek ways to address the threats; we want to do something, anything. But too often what we do is wasteful and time consuming. His analysis builds on Max Weber's classic study on 'The Protestant Ethic and the Spirit of Capitalism' to which we have already referred.

Weber realised that the huge growth of the industrial revolution could not be explained by technological development alone. Such development was a necessary but insufficient condition for such growth. People needed to be motivated as well, they needed reasons to work long hours, to save, to invest and to plan for the future. Weber concluded that these reasons could be found in the profound uncertainty they faced about the fundamental realities of life because of their Puritan religious beliefs. Wuthnow analyses the responses that have been made to the nuclear threat, the international terrorism, weapons of mass destruction, pandemics such as bird flu and swine flu and environmental catastrophe. In each case he found that the response to an impending crisis was to take very high levels of action. But the problem is that very often the action is inappropriate and, to make matters worse, those responses are institutionalised in independent, relatively unaccountable organisations established to drive the response. According to Wuthnow

> "The bias for action encourages people to act, but does not dictate exactly how they will act. That part is shaped more by what they have heard and learned about previous crises. If they learned that a big nuclear build-up during the Cold War was what saved the nation from annihilation, they are likely to imagine that a huge military budget will be the best way to deter terrorists". (Wuthnow, 2010:215)

Significant amounts of money have been spent specifically monitoring and preventing dangers that have been identified. Such levels of expenditure highlight why it is important to get the response right. Ireland has seen a classic example of failure in this respect. The Irish Government's response to the banking crisis of 2008 was on a huge scale and involved massive expenditure but it is generally agreed that it was based on poor analysis, was an over-reaction that resulted in excessive expenditure and additional damage being done. Action had been required but the action taken was very problematic and will have costs and consequences for Irish citizens for decades.

Reflecting on these situations we acknowledge that action is required to deal with situations that emerge. In particular action is required in addressing the challenges posed by major threats such as those identified above. However the lack of a clear social analysis, the failure to identify the consequences of actions taken, and the failure to address basic questions concerning meaning, concerning the future, concerning purpose, through sustained philosophical or theological reflection point to fundamental weaknesses that are likely to accompany inadequately thought-through responses. People jump into action because they convince themselves that engaging in such action is the best approach. But it is important that when actions are taken that they be as near as possible to the right actions. Very often mistakes are made because people base their action on what was done before. Governments are especially prone to this failure but many people make the same mistake. To counteract this tendency it is crucial that as many as possible be involved in providing social analysis and envisioning the future, in recognizing and addressing basic questions about values and meaning. The institutions created to address major problems should always be involved in these processes but so should those impacted on by decisions taken; these should always have their voice heard and their perspective included in this process. A sharing of responsibility is essential in these situations.

1.4 To link rights and responsibilities

There is an urgent need to have a calm and open discussion about the relationship between rights and responsibilities. From a historical perspective it is interesting to recall that

"In the debate on human rights in the French Revolutionary Parliament of 1789 the demand was made: if a declaration of the rights of man is proclaimed, it must be combined with a declaration of the responsibilities of man. Otherwise, in the end all human beings would have only rights which they would play off against others, and no one would any longer recognise the responsibilities without which the rights cannot function". (Kung, 1997:99)[61]

In more recent times Professor Jim Ife[62] noted that,

"One of the important aspects of human rights is that they are linked to human responsibilities. This has been a link that many have sought to deny or at least to minimise. For those on the political right, the idea of rights is regarded with some suspicion if not downright hostility, unless understood within very narrow liberal confines of individual freedom rights and property rights; anything beyond that, such as the right to education, health, housing, employment, job security, working conditions, income security and a clean environment sounds dangerously like socialism. For such people, responsibilities are much more important, and are the key to a stable society. To those in the political left, however, it is rights that are seen as important, while the idea of responsibility sounds like paternalism, social control and "mutual obligation" with all its punitive overtones.

"This political polarisation of rights and responsibilities has meant that many people, because of their ideological blinkers, do not treat both seriously, and choose to concentrate on one at the expense of the other, and this has resulted in something of a gap in human rights theorising. Yet the connection between rights and responsibilities is obvious. If I have a right, then that implies a responsibility on the part of some other person, group or institution to (i) allow me the freedom to exercise

---

[61] In 1992 the Commission on Global Governance was established by the United Nations Organisation. Its report published in 1995 is entitled *"Our Global Neighbourhood"*,
[62] 2004, A paper delivered to a conference on Community Development, Human Rights and the Grassroots in Deakin University, *Linking Community Development and Human Rights.*

that right, (ii) provide the mechanisms to protect that right, and/or (iii) make positive provision so that my right can be realised. The responsibilities associated with rights may lie with other individuals, with groups, with communities, or with governments. For example, the right to education requires some level of state action or policy to provide adequate educational institutions and structures, either by itself, or to ensure that others do it."

Ife goes on to say,

"The responsibilities associated with human rights are often the most contentious part of rights discourse. We may readily agree on statements of rights, for example as described in the Universal Declaration, but when it comes to deciding whose responsibility it is to ensure the protection and realisation of those rights there can be major disagreement, for example, who should be responsible for ensuring our rights to health care are met: the Federal Government, the State Government, the private market, employers, the community, the family, or the individual her/himself? In reality the answer will usually be some combination of most or all of these, but then the question becomes what is the appropriate combination, and how much should each contribute? Responsibilities are usually more contentious than rights, and it is interesting to note that we seem to find it easier to draw up charters of rights than we do charters of responsibilities. Perhaps it is more appropriate to call human rights workers human responsibilities workers, as it is more often the responsibilities that are in question, and that need to be established.

"The necessary link between rights and responsibilities is the first indication that community might be important in human rights. The strict individualist notion of rights – "my rights" – makes no sense. A sole individual on a desert island has no rights – because there is nobody to recognise them and to accept the responsibilities that flow from them. Rights require some sort of group, community, collective or society, which is held together by a series of interlocking and reciprocal rights and responsibilities. For this reason it is better to talk about "our rights" rather than the more traditional western liberal notion of "my rights". (Ife, 2004:2)

Like Ife, Kung noted that "hardly ever has it been stated in an official international document that concrete responsibilities, human responsibilities, are associated with human rights". Kung goes on to quote the report (Commission on Global Governance, 1995):

"At the same time, all people share a responsibility to:
- contribute to the common good;
- consider the impact of their actions on the security and welfare of others;
- promote equity, including gender equity;
- protect the interests of future generation by pursuing sustainable development and safeguarding the global commons;
- preserve humanity's cultural and intellectual heritage;
- be active participants in governance; and
- work to eliminate corruption. (Quoted in Kung, 1997:226)

Kung discusses the relationship of law with rights and responsibilities and concludes that:

No comprehensive ethic of humanity can be derived from human rights alone, fundamental though these are for human beings; it must also cover the human responsibilities which were there before the law. Before any codification in law and any state legislation there is the moral independence and conscious self- responsibility of the individual, with which not only elementary rights but also elementary responsibilities are connected" (Kung, 1997:103)

One of the responsibilities that attaches to a right is the responsibility to exercise that right. There is no point in having the right to freedom of expression, or the right to education, or the right to vote, or the right to join a trade union, if nobody bothers to exercise that right…A society that respects and values human rights is one where people are encouraged to exercise their rights, and accept a responsibility to do so where they can. This is an active participatory society, that requires citizens to be active contributors rather than passive consumers; and the promotion of such a participatory society has long been the agenda of community development. (Ife, 2004:3)

Ife argues that all human rights have both individual and collective dimensions. He goes on to say,

We also need to apply the same reasoning to the other side of the equation, namely responsibilities, and to insist that there should be both individual and collective understandings of responsibilities, duties or obligations. Responsibilities do not lie only with individuals, but to say this does not invalidate any notion of individual responsibility. Across both the rights and responsibilities dimensions, therefore, we can consider the relative place of individual and collective understandings. Here we are inevitably affected in our analysis by ideological factors, and different ideologies or value systems will suggest that the balance between individual and collective rights and responsibilities be understood in different ways. (Ife, 2004:7)

In Ireland there has been much discussion along the lines outlined here. In these discussions some have emphasised responsibilities while others focused on rights. There was much argument when Government substantially reduced the funding for various Human Rights bodies. There was also discussion concerning whether or not various human rights instruments such as the Universal Charter are being respected. There has been a fairly broad acceptance of political and civil rights but much dispute concerning social, economic and cultural rights. An example of the latter can be found in the endless discussion about how to address unemployment.

People have a right to work yet for much of its history Ireland has been unable to provide paid employment for many of its citizens. While the right to work is not contested there has rarely been a discussion on where the responsibility to provide work lies. The question of how people's right to work can be secured if there are insufficient paid jobs available is not addressed by most commentators. There has also been a profound failure to recognise that much work is being done but is not paid employment. Much work done in the home, in the community, in the wider society, in the development of people themselves, is unpaid but is real work. There is an urgent need to take a much more imaginative approach to ensuring that people have meaningful work and sufficient income to live with dignity when paid jobs are not available for all who seek paid employment. The introduction of a Basic Income system and the recognition of work that is not paid employment could form two components of such a strategy. Instead of seeking creative ways in which rights such as these could be honoured Ireland has seen much fruitless debate focused on blaming different institutions (government, employers, etc.) for not honouring their 'responsibilities' to produce jobs for all. The authors strongly believe that social, economic and cultural rights should be respected and delivered. But creative approaches would be required to secure these rights in practice. We believe that such approaches are much more likely to be identified, promoted and acted on if there was a much broader engagement of all groups in Irish society, especially by those who are most affected by the reality of unemployment. Such a process, if it was genuinely deliberative, would be much more likely to ensure that rights and responsibilities were recognised, balanced and vindicated.[63]

1.5 To work towards a new paradigm more appropriate for the 21st century[64]

A further reason that responsibility in shaping the future needs to be shared far more widely has to do with the need to develop a new paradigm of development for our world, a paradigm that is more appropriate for the 21st century. We live in a world that promotes constant economic growth.

---

[63] These issues have been addressed by the authors in a wide range of publications. Some are listed in the references at the end of this chapter.

[64] Much of this section draws on our previous work. The references are contained at the end of this paper. Our most recent work on this will be elaborated in a forthcoming edition of *Trends in Social Cohesion* to be published by the Council of Europe.

The world's present development model requires constant, economic growth and without growth the wheels come off as has been obvious in the period following the 2007 economic upheaval. In previous published work we have pointed out that conventional economic wisdom argues that continuing on an economic growth path for the foreseeable future will produce a world where everyone has a stake and where the good life can be accessed by all (for example, cf. Healy/Reynolds 2006, 1993). It is presumed that everyone, in a world population twice as large as now, can reasonably aspire to and achieve the high-consumption lifestyle enjoyed by the world's affluent minority at present. This is seen as progress.

This conventional economic vision of the future is unattainable, however. Environmental degradation, encroaching deserts, unemployment, starvation, widening gaps between rich and poor, exclusion from participation in either decision-making or development of society, these are the global realities confronting decision-makers today. Economic globalisation and environmental stress are accompanied by social inequality, endemic deprivation, an unstable financial system, social unrest and violence. Millions of people in the richer parts of the world recognise these problems and are seriously concerned about the plight of the billions of people on all continents whose lived experience is one of constant exclusion from the resources and the power that shape this world.

People feel powerless. The media present one vision of the future and assume it is the only desirable or viable future. Politicians, more concerned about the next election, rarely discuss the fundamental causes of, or long-term solutions to, the issues and problems they confront every day. It is crucial that questions be asked concerning the world's future and particularly, how a viable, sustainable, desirable future can be attained.

Previously we argued that the source of many of the problems the world currently faces lies in the development paradigm being followed and in its view of progress (Healy/Reynolds 1993; 2006:2-8). Capra generalised Kuhn's definition of a scientific paradigm to that of a social paradigm, which he defined as 'a constellation of concepts, values, perceptions, and practices shared by a community, which forms a particular vision of reality that is the basis of the way the community organises itself.' (Capra 1996)

A paradigm contains core beliefs and assumptions. It is a model or framework from which analyses, decisions and actions flow. 'The world is flat' is a good example of a paradigm. If one accepts this, then one holds certain values, takes certain actions and expects certain results. On the other hand if one's paradigm is that 'the world is round' then one holds different values, takes different actions and seeks very different results. Moving from a framework which sees the world as flat to one that sees the world as round is a paradigm shift.

Paradigms are extremely powerful as they determine one's 'world view'. They underpin decisions concerning what constitutes a problem, how it should be approached, what action should be taken and what the desired outcome might be (Healy and Reynolds, 1993). History shows that if a paradigm is producing negative results, however, it is not always changed immediately. Thomas Kuhn (Kuhn, 1970) analysed how paradigm change was effected in the natural sciences. Changes did not occur through a process of cumulative research which brought people ever closer to a final solution to the problems encountered. "Rather it happened through a 'revolution' in which a small group of scientists recognise that the existing frame of reference is inadequate for the resolution of newly emerging problems" (McCabe 1996). They seek out a new paradigm. Change, however, is resisted and the transition is never smooth (Dunne, 1991). As the existing paradigm becomes more recognisably inadequate the new one attracts more and more support until the old one is finally abandoned. Tension and conflict are usually part of the transition process as are rearguard actions in defence of the outdated paradigm. Total acceptance of the new paradigm can take a long time as was the case for example in the world of science in the shift from the Copernican paradigm to the Newtonian one and again in the later shift to the Einsteinian one.

We believe that resistance to change at present fits into this pattern. Much time is being consumed defending an outdated and discredited paradigm.

The old paradigm is broken. A new one is needed urgently. All members of society should be encouraged to participate in the formulation of this new paradigm. Decisions on the shape of the future should be open to all groups in society so that subsequently responsibility will be shared among all stakeholders and not be confined to any one grouping in society.

1.6 To protect the interests of future generations

One group that has no voice at moments of great challenge and change, such as the present, is the next generation. Yet their voice must be heard in this context. Many of the decisions made in today's world will have significant impacts on people not alive today. The level of debt we take on, the education systems we support, the damage we do to the environment, these are just a few examples of areas where we are making decisions that will hugely impact on future generations. The chapter in this book written by Mary Cunningham raises key issues in this area. Here we wish simply to highlight a few items we consider to be of crucial importance on this issue. The Brundtland report entitled 'Our Common Future' published in 1987 by the World Commission on Environment and Development, warned that the world was living on the credit of future generations. (WCED, 1987) In the decades since this report was published the world has become much more conscious of the destruction of the world's eco-systems, the reality of climate change and the impact these and similar developments are having on the sustainability of the planet. The limits to growth are being recognised more clearly. Slowly but surely there is an emerging recognition of the need to consider the rights of future generations when decisions are being made.

A decade later the United National Educational, Scientific and Cultural Organisation (UNESCO) in 1997 produced the *Declaration on the Responsibilities of the Present Generations towards Future Generations*. It opens with the statement: "The present generations have the responsibility of ensuring that the needs and interests of present and future generations are fully safeguarded". It has articles on freedom of choice, maintenance and perpetuation of humankind, preservation of life on Earth, protection of the environment, human genome and biodiversity, cultural diversity and cultural heritage, common heritage of humankind, peace, development and education, non-discrimination and implementation. We list these here to highlight the range of issues that must be addressed if future generations are to be protected at the present time.

Interestingly enough this declaration has not been ratified. Most of the discussion on these issues and their implications for future generations takes place in the disciplines of philosophy and law. It is clear that, in a world dominated by an individualist world view, consideration of future generations has not been a priority. Likewise, in a democratic system, citizens of the future don't have a vote so their voice is most rarely heard. Both of these problems are exacerbated by the short-termism that characterises most political processes in the modern world. There is great institutional and cultural inertia on this issue. Maja Gopel has proposed that "if we wish to strengthen a long-term point of view in our current institutions, a good solution would be the creation of guardians for future generations." (Gopel, 2011:105). She points out that actual progress on policies that would protect future generations are rare, arguing that "We have built institutions that encapsulate extreme competitiveness and individualism, but also a structural short-termism. Thus, even if individual actors are convinced of the ethics of obligations to future generations, it is very difficult to act on it." (ibid) She points out that some governments are now establishing institutions that seek to provide a perspective of intergenerational equity, institutions such as parliamentary committees, commissioners and ombudspersons who analyse policy proposals from a long-term, perspective. Some of these have an advocacy role.

Given these realities it seems very sensible that a voice for future generations be part of decision-making processes today. They, more than most, have an interest in how this world develops in the decades and centuries ahead.

Conclusion to section 1

We have identified six areas which demonstrate why responsibility for shaping the future should be shared. This list is by no means exhaustive.

Given these developments and reflections and the scale of the challenges currently emerging there is a profound need to empower all members of society to share responsibility for shaping the future. There is a growing recognition that governments cannot do everything required to secure the common good and ensure the well-being of all. Likewise there is a growing realisation that markets cannot be relied on to achieve both these outcomes. There is an urgent need for new approaches to governance, regulation, conflict management and redistribution of resources which enable all to contribute to developing and working towards a viable vision for the future.

There is also a need to restore the ability of public institutions to rectify democratic deficits and to settle social and distributive conflicts. To achieve these ends there is a need to develop effective forms of dialogue based on an impartial search for the common good and the well-being of all, It is crucial that agreements made are fair and just and that those who are poor and/or vulnerable are recognised and protected from the harmful consequences of decisions in which they have had no part. The world is dominated by economic, political and technological forces that work closely together for their mutual benefit and very often at the cost of the ordinary citizen. These trends will continue and issues such as the common good and the well-being of all will not gain their rightful place on the world's agenda unless decision-making includes the voices and perspectives of all those impacted on by the decisions made. The case for sharing responsibility in shaping the future is very strong. What is not so clear is what this entails. We now move on to address this issue.

2. HOW?

If responsibility for shaping the future is to be shared then many issues arise concerning how this is to be done. We now address seven of these issues here. These are:

- Requirements if responsibility for shaping the future is to be shared
- Deliberative democracy

- Government – What is required of Government?
- Social Partnership in Ireland
- The local level
- The Corporate Sector
- The Community and Voluntary Sector

2.1 Requirements if responsibility for shaping the future is to be shared

The Draft 'Charter on Shared Social Responsibilities'[65] being considered by the Council of Europe provides an excellent summary of the fundamentals that are required if responsibility is to be shared in a fair and just manner. It states:

An effective strategy in the field of shared social responsibilities presupposes:

a. recognition of the full range of stakeholders, their demands and possible contributions in terms of action or suggestions, their rights and obligations, and their role in a social system based on close interdependencies;
b. deliberative processes, making it possible to refine the preferences of the stakeholders and establish priorities through exchanges of different arguments and viewpoints and through the impartial arbitration of differing interests;
c. multi-stakeholder, multi-level and multi-sectoral innovation and skill and knowledge-acquisition processes making it possible for all involved to evaluate the consistency between the decisions taken and the European frames of reference in the field of fundamental rights, and paving the way for the equitable and democratic management of common goods;
d. forms of partnership and governance broadly involving the stakeholders at different levels and making it possible for a plurality of players to become involved and co-operate in a sustainable way;

---
[65] The full text of this Draft is contained at the beginning of this publication.

e. institutional mechanisms offering confidence in the fact that each partner will act in accordance with the decisions taken and will refrain from any harmful behaviour or acting solely in his or her own interest to the detriment of the interests of others;

g. recognition of material and non-material common goods. Among the objects of rights, common goods are those which express a functional utility for the exercise of fundamental rights and the development of the individual, and which contribute to the feeling of belonging to the human race. Common goods include natural resources, the cultural and historic heritage, social protection, social cohesion, democratic institutions and the sharing of knowledge.

In a footnote it adds:

"Proximity is a crucial factor. Within regions, towns, neighbourhoods, local institutions, public services, enterprises and the work place it is possible to bring together all the stakeholders required to share social responsibilities. Proximity also encourages the setting up of partnerships and networks, strengthening reciprocity and the stakeholders' confidence in joint action."

These fundamental requirements sit very well with the parameters set out in part one of this chapter. We wish to reflect a little on one of the critically important requirements identified by the Council of Europe above i.e. "deliberative processes, making it possible to refine the preferences of the stakeholders and establish priorities through exchanges of different arguments and viewpoints and through the impartial arbitration of differing interests".

2.2 Deliberative democracy

The idea of deliberative democracy goes back millennia. However, its modern support springs from the idea that for a Government to be legitimate it must embody the will of the people. It adopts elements of both representative democracy and direct democracy and differs from traditional democratic theory in that deliberation, not voting, is the primary source of a law's legitimacy. How such a process is to be carried out in practice has been discussed extensively. There is no such thing as a common good on which everyone would agree so some have argued that governance and decision-making should be left with leadership elites. However most would agree that political engagement requires citizens to have some focus on the common good when making decisions.

In terms of sharing responsibility in shaping the future the authors believe that without a 'deliberative democracy' process there will be little real sharing of responsibility and little focus on the common good. A deliberative decision making process is one where all stakeholders are involved but the power differentials are removed. In such a process stakeholders are involved in the framing, implementing and evaluating of policies and measures that impact on them. Given the analysis provided in the first part of this paper it is clear that there are many reasons why responsibility in shaping the future should be shared. However, for that to be achieved a deliberative process is required. We agree with the Council of Europe's assessment that "the failure to take adequate account of the possible areas of complementarity between representative democracy, deliberative democracy and participatory democracy acts as a break on innovation in all fields in which the reciprocal nature of commitments and joint decision-making based on impartial reasoning are essential in order to guarantee the principles of social, environmental and intergenerational justice." A deliberative approach is also recommended by the Council of Europe in its Social Cohesion Plan launched in 2010.

Elster claims that a deliberative approach would produce better outcomes for four reasons. These are:

1. The emphasis placed on open dialogue may unlock untapped knowledge about the strengths and weaknesses of existing methods of doing things.
2. Those involved in the policy-making process have the opportunity to acquire new skills and greater know-how about particular policy methods.
3. The promotion of collaborative and joint action may induce a richer

mode of decision making, by encouraging participants to justify the positions they adopt with high quality reasoning. More informed, better thought-out decisions not only foster shared understandings between the different participants, but also deepen the wider legitimacy of policies.
4. The encouragement of consensus building and trust-enhancing modes of interaction may atrophy the boundaries between the different constituencies that are involved in a policy network. New relationships of interdependence may emerge that strengthen the collaborative ethos of the process. (Elster 1998)

Deliberative processes do not displace representative democracy; rather, they have the capacity to strengthen it and should be seen as an essential and complementary approach which brings citizens, stakeholders and public authorities into closer alignment. Using a deliberative process makes it possible for everyone to put forward their own visions and subsequently to reformulate their preferences in light of the discussions, analysis and testing of views that takes place. In this way all can contribute to the development of shared knowledge, shared objectives and shared projects. According to the Council of Europe's draft Charter, a deliberative process would:

a. bring to the fore and examine in a public, transparent setting the different interests put forward by citizens and stakeholders highlighting their interrelations;
b. reconcile individual preferences and demands with common priorities in the field of social, environmental and intergenerational justice and the well-being of all and reach agreements acceptable to each stakeholder;
c. construct shared visions and knowledge capable of reconciling the aspirations of present and future generations;
d. conclude agreements acknowledged as being fair and which will encourage each stakeholder to honour and implement them in practice;
e. reduce imbalances of power between strong and weak stakeholders on the construction of knowledge and on decision-making;

f. renew the sense of specific responsibilities and broadening the scope of individual and collective choices;
g. reactivate the stakeholders' moral and social resources, forms of collective intelligence and democratic skills;
h. highlight the key role of social citizenship in countering the fragmentation of responsibilities of individuals as workers, consumers, savers, investors, etc.; (Charter: Section 20)

To achieve this the Council of Europe suggests that deliberative processes must be structured in accordance with well-defined methodological principles. They claim that each stakeholder must be able to:

a. interact on an equal footing with other stakeholders, all present and duly represented;
b. have an equal right to information and freedom of expression;
c. hear the viewpoint of others in the context of impartial discussions, seeking a consensus that is as equitable as possible;
d. take part in choosing alternatives and taking decisions;
e. discuss differences of opinion openly and publicise the agreements reached;
f. clarify and take into account the long-term effects and interests of decisions on objectives and means of action, including their impact on the weaker players and on future generations;
g. make commitments and receive guarantees about the implementation of decisions and the respective contributions of the other stakeholders;
h. take part in the construction of criteria to assess decisions and initiatives regarding the well-being of all and in the design and implementation of evaluation procedures. (Charter: section 21)

The authors believe that a deliberative process is essential if there is to be a sharing of responsibility in shaping the future. We agree with the Council of Europe's draft Charter which identifies the core elements of such a deliberative process.

2.3 Government

2.3.1 Initiatives at national Government level

Governments, for the most part, are well aware of the growing interdependence of the various institutions in their countries and beyond. They also realise that the impact of actions taken by people or institutions have far-reaching effects. Consequently, they have tried in a variety of ways to involve various stakeholders.

One type of approach has been to involve all the key actors addressing a particular area of policy such as health or poverty or energy. Views are sought from all stakeholders and discussed. Some decisions may be made by those participating in this process. Such decisions tend to focus on actions to be taken by participants in the process. However, this process is most often limited by a set of parameters set by Government that may not be breached. The group may well believe, for example, that a particular approach to a problem may be most effective but if that approach is outside the parameters set then it may not be pursued. On the other hand the group may make proposals for Government action but these proposals may be ignored by Government for ideological or other reasons.

A second type of approach involves actors who are equal such as nation states. Authority does not rest with any particular individual participant. These draw together the information on the particular issue being discussed and make decisions on what is to be done. One example of this would be the development of the United Nations Millennium Development Goals (MDGs). In response to the challenges faced by the Third World the UN Millennium Declaration was adopted in 2000 at the largest-ever gathering of heads of state. It committed countries - both rich and poor - to doing all they could to eradicate poverty, promote human dignity and equality and achieve peace, democracy and environmental sustainability. World leaders promised to work together to meet concrete targets for advancing development and reducing poverty by 2015 or earlier. Emanating from the Millennium Declaration, a set of Millennium Development Goals was agreed. These bind countries to do more in the attack on inadequate incomes, widespread hunger, gender inequality, environmental deterioration and lack of education, healthcare and clean water. They also include actions to reduce debt and increase aid, trade and technology transfers to poor countries. Some countries took these commitments very seriously, others simply ignored them. Progress on achieving the MDGs has been far behind schedule.

A third type of approach at national Government level is the sharing of responsibility by means of a contract between the stakeholders involved. One example of this is the Shared Responsibility Agreements between the Australian Government and Indigenous Communities in Australia. The Government's responsibility is to provide services, including infrastructure. The Aboriginal communities' responsibility is to identify the issues they want to address and what they will do in response to the Government's investment. [66]

The fourth type of approach is the engagement of different parts of the same entity such as Government departments in the discussion of a particular issue. In Ireland, the establishment of a Senior Officials Group on Social Inclusion (SOGSI) to ensure coherence and increased capacity in Government's response to the various problems posed by social exclusion. It is an attempt to manage the sharing of responsibility between different Government departments. This approach to sharing responsibility may be effective at times but unless it's very well managed it can easily lead to a diffusion of responsibility to a point where there is no real accountability.

A fifth approach to sharing responsibility is the engagement by Government of the various sectors of society in a process aimed at producing a national agreement on a wide range of policy areas over a period of time. This is a far larger and challenging enterprise. In Ireland this approach was used to produce a series of national agreements starting in 1987 with the most recent, signed in 2006, setting out a series of 23 high-level goals to be achieved over a 10-year period. Detailed proposals for implementation were set out for the initial years of this agreement.

---

[66] These issues are addressed in a much more detailed way by Arne Scholz in Scholz: 2011.

Ireland's economic crisis intervened however. Government continued to use this structure to address issues of pay and conditions. However, it has tended to approach issues of social policy in a different manner during the crisis. We shall return to this particular structure later in this paper.

2.3.2 What is required of Government at national level

If there is to be a real sharing of responsibility in shaping the future then Government has a responsibility to make this happen. What does that require of Government? The Council of Europe's draft Charter sets out what it considers to be required of Government as follows:

State and governmental authorities are encouraged to promote the sharing of social responsibilities by adopting appropriate legal rules. To this end, they are required to

a. encourage and legitimise forums for negotiation and discussion between the many stakeholders;
b. motivate stakeholders to comply with the principles relating to the sharing of social responsibilities and the implementation of decisions;
c. make interaction with stakeholders a key opportunity for learning, so that representative democracy and deliberative democracy become mutually reinforcing;
d. communicate information so as to explain the thinking behind public policies enabling a sharing of social responsibilities, and to encourage action to that end;
e. where convincing data are available, promote and publicise the positive results of innovation in the field of social, environmental and intergenerational justice
f. set up institutions specialising in mediation and conflict resolution, facilitating the exercise of shared social responsibility;
g. reassess the role of public servants as mediators between different stakeholders who may have different interests, bearing in mind the constitutional principles and democratic procedures in force;
h. encourage multi-lateral and cross-border activities, including the networking of territories committed to implementing the Council

of Europe's Action Plan for Social Cohesion;
i. exchange, develop and codify positive results, in the context of the Council of Europe and with other international organisations.

These appear to the authors to be a comprehensive list of what is required of the State and of Government. The need to legitimise this process is crucial. So too is the need to learn from stakeholders in the process as it develops. A deliberative process is the best protection against taking inappropriate precipitous action that a more reflective process would guard against. Ensuring such a process takes place is of real benefit to Government. The obligation on Government to establish institutions facilitating the exercise of shared responsibility would also be a welcome development. Taking action along the lines identified above would also be likely to result in the problems underpinning the current dominant paradigm of development being exposed and a more appropriate paradigm being adopted.

2.4 Social Partnership in Ireland

We have already referred to Ireland's social partnership process. It draws together five 'pillars' of social partners i.e. employers, trade unions, farming organisations, community and voluntary sector organisations, and environmental organisations. These have worked with Government over the years to produce national agreements. As noted already Ireland's economic crisis intervened. Government continued to use this structure to address issues of pay and conditions. However, it has tended to approach issues of social policy in a different manner during the crisis.

Social partnership was a major development in governance in Ireland. The basis of social partnership was a process of shared reflection, analysis and policy development followed by negotiations within mutually understood frameworks. The National Economic and Social Council (NESC) played a crucial role in this process, on each occasion producing a strategy document to form the basis of the subsequent negotiations. Once an agreement was in place the monitoring process facilitated the involvement of the social partners in the on-going implementation of the commitments contained in the agreement.

This process produced a substantial network of policy design, monitoring and evaluation involving both government and social partners. In theory there was a concerted effort to apply the policy learning developed at a strategic and national level to a wide range of problems that had been identified. In practice this did not always happen. We have documented this in some details in a range of other publications (e.g. Healy/Reynolds, 2002). This process involved substantial levels of civic engagement by a wide range of actors. Their voices were heard to a greater or lesser degree in various arenas on a wide range of policy issues. The inclusion of the Community and Voluntary Sector in this process in 1996 was significant in this regards. So too was the inclusion of the Environmental Pillar a decade later.

A major issue that was raised from time to time concerned the role of the Oireachtas (Parliament) in the social partnership process. Some argued that the exclusion of elected deputies and senators from the process was a drawback. This is a viewpoint with which we agree. At the same time we reject the claim sometimes made that social partnership in Ireland undermined the democratic process. Such a claim fails to appreciate the process through which these national agreements were developed. The agreements were signed off by the pillars of social partners and by the Government. There would be no national agreement unless the Government of the day signed off on the agreement. The Government is the choice of the electorate. They have the final say on whether or not a national agreement is to be implemented. Consequently, to claim that those who were the elected choice of the people were excluded from the social partnership process is simply untrue. However we argued for years that further involvement of the Oireachtas would be desirable and we made proposals on how that might be achieved.

The democratic consequences of social partnership in Ireland have been interpreted in two broad ways. One view is that social partnership has been a malign influence on Irish democracy as it undermines the role of representative democracy and, in particular, elected politicians. The other view is that social partnership has enriched Irish democracy by deepening deliberative democracy in the country. The authors believe that the social partnership process meets many of the challenges posed in trying to develop a deliberative democratic process. However we also believe that the deliberative nature of the process was not always honoured by Government or by some members of the Pillars engaged in the process. There were many occasions when the power differentials were very obvious and the weak and vulnerable were not always protected as they should have been in such a process.

A social partnership process that operated in a genuinely deliberative manner would go a long way towards strengthening governance in Ireland. It would also provide protection against any repetition of Ireland's recent series of crises. Not alone would it have to be real deliberation, it would have to be seen to be a real deliberative process. Since its inception in 1987 the social partnership process has adapted to the demands placed on it as Ireland's development and the reality of the wider world experienced seismic change. To become a genuinely deliberative process that would meet the criteria identified in this paper would require some changes to the processes involved. It would also require a change in mindset among participants. The authors believe both of these requirements can be met. However it should not be the only deliberative mechanism in Ireland's governance structure.

Deliberative democracy should be a characteristic of governance at all levels of government and across other sectors as well. We now take a short look at some of these other areas where deliberative processes are desirable and do-able.

2.5. The Local Level

Deliberative democracy can also be applied at local level. Denters noted that "With regard to local development the deliberative governance framework promotes a form of networked governance which involves local inclusive bodies engaging in problem-solving activities to the betterment of disadvantaged communities and groups in the area". (Denters, 2003) The Council of Europe's draft Charter on Shared Social Responsibilities sets out some very useful guidelines on what is required of municipal, local and regional governments. In Aricle 11 it states:

> Local and regional authorities, and especially, city, neighbourhood and village authorities, are encouraged to promote the sharing of social responsibilities. To this end, they are required to:
>
> a. strengthen consistency between the objectives of social, environmental and intergenerational justice, decided by common accord, and individual and institutional choices;
> b. introduce mechanisms of participatory and deliberative governance, making possible the sharing of social responsibilities;
> c. conclude agreements with other administrative tiers facilitating the establishment of local participatory structures;
> d. foster the involvement of residents in projects of general interest, through the preservation and enhancement of common goods, the landscape, the cultural heritage and all local resources contributing to the strengthening of capital, motivations and shared confidence, while including the diversity resulting from immigration;
> e. frame local policies which acknowledge and take into account the contribution made by everyone to strengthening social protection and social cohesion, the fair allocation of common goods, the formation of the principles of social, environmental and intergenerational justice and which also ensure that all stakeholders have a negotiation and decision-making power.

Many local areas in Ireland have local partnerships in place. These vary in terms of the areas and issues addressed. Where there has been a genuinely deliberative process in place they have been very successful. The Northside Partnership in Dublin is a good example of this in practice in an urban area. IRD (Integrated Rural Development) Duhallow is a good rural example. There are many more examples that could be cited. All of these are community-based development organisations that combine the efforts and resources of state bodies, local authorities, local communities and individual entrepreneurs for the benefit of the local areas. These partnerships establish and support initiatives directed towards the generation of enterprise for the benefit and welfare of communities in their areas who may be deprived for whatever reason. An interesting part of their approach is that they support geographically based communities but they also support issue-based groups focusing on issues such as youth, women, lone parents, mental health, sport, education, culture, the environmental and many more. A regrettable part of recent Government policy in Ireland has been a series of initiatives that forced the amalgamation of partnerships without the willing agreement of many and with little real dialogue. In some cases such amalgamation may have been a positive move. Overall however the approach was a real failure of government to respect a deliberative process that, in many cases, if it had been given the opportunity would have found much better solutions to the problems identified by Government.

2.6. Corporate Sector

The corporate sector is another area where deliberative processes would have a positive impact. Companies' activities often have big impacts on social, environmental and intergenerational justice. In their search for competitive advantage they may well ignore the values and needs of local communities. The corporate sector has developed the area of 'corporate social responsibility' (CSR) to keep these issues on its agenda when decisions are made. However there are many doubts concerning CSR. Companies see CSR as part of their marketing and branding strategies. They argue that 'doing well by doing good' is a good approach to which they subscribe. However there is little accountability in terms of how companies select their CSR priorities. Likewise they are not answerable in any meaningful way concerning the quality and continuity of services they provide; they are totally free to discontinue services whenever they see fit.

In this context the Council of Europe's Draft Charter states:

> Companies are encouraged to adapt their forms of governance to incorporate the general principles of shared social responsibility, so as to:

a. rethink their aims and operational principles in a context of social, environmental and intergenerational justice, bearing in mind all the costs and impacts of their activity;
b. seek lasting competitive advantages by taking into account societal values and social and ecological needs and adapting production processes, rather than focusing exclusively on reducing labour force costs and the socialisation of environmental harm;
c. comply with national legislation concerning working conditions and make sure they are compatible with international working standards in force;
d. integrate further in decision-making the viewpoints of workers, consumers, those who experience the harmful consequences of production, institutions and the relevant civil society organisations;
e. develop ways of managing relationships and conflicts, both in-house and with the stakeholders in the communities and areas where they are located, in a spirit of dialogue, confidence and mutual respect.
f. make the life cycle of products transparent, from the origin of the raw materials to the management of waste;
g. publish periodic reports on the social and environmental impact of their activities, including those of a financial nature;

Any reasonable analysis of the world's crises in the period 2007 and following would recognise the major role the corporate sector played in causing these crises. Development of an approach along these lines would mark real progress.

2.7. The Community and Voluntary Sector

A healthy and vibrant Community and Voluntary (CV) sector is an essential component of any modern democracy. Effective, democratic governance in the twenty first century requires active engagement from all parts of society. One of the contributions the Community and Voluntary Sector makes is towards maintaining the essential balance between the government and its services on the one hand and the market on the other hand.

Such a safe space between the state and the market could be an enabling framework that would allow people to address a range of issues. Civil society is not there to replace the state or its institutions. The chapter by Ivan Cooper in this publication addresses the potential of the CV sector to play a meaningful role in the coproduction of public services and to ensure positive outcomes are produced. But the production of services is only one of the many areas in which the CV sector is involved. It also plays a key role in areas such as social analysis, advocacy, developing, monitoring and evaluating policy and many more. In the process of social partnership already discussed in this chapter the CV sector the CV Pillar played a substantial role from its inclusion in the process in 1996.

The Council of Europe's draft Charter sets out what it believes this sector and the trade union sector should do. It states:

> Trade unions, associations and non-governmental organisations are encouraged to participate in the sharing of social responsibilities. To this end, they are required to:

a. incorporate the principles of shared social responsibility in their aims and organisational structure;
b. take part in forums for deliberative and participatory democracy which enable shared social responsibility to be exercised;
c. take part in multi-stakeholder, multi-level and multi-sectoral processes;
d. exercise, particularly in the case of trade unions, the right to be informed and consulted and defend the employment rights established by the ILO;
e. subscribe, particularly in the case of NGOs, to the code of good practice for civil participation in the decision-making process, adopted by the Council of Europe's Conference of INGOs on 1 October 2009 [CONF/PLE(2009)Code1].

Many organisations and bodies within the CV sector already espouse a deliberative approach in their working. Many have developed methodologies they follow to make such an approach a reality. Anna

Coote (Coote: 2011) has set out some very useful practical guidelines drawing on work done with healthcare organisations in the UK. She lists the following ground rules for engagement:

- Know what you can change and be sure you can take account of what people say.
- Engage early and plan ahead; find out who is likely to be affected and who is supposed to benefit.
- Embed engagement in the work process so that service users and the public are informed and involved at all key stages.
- Include all the right people and make special efforts to reach out to those whose voices are seldom heard.
- Choose your methods to suit your purpose by being clear what it is you are trying to achieve.
- Provide clear information so that people have all they need to participate in a discussion.
- Make sure you have adequate resources and time, and work out where your resources will come from.
- Keep things in proportion so that the scale of the project fits your timescale and budget.
- Act on what you learn so that what matters most to service users and the public informs and shapes your work.
- Always give feedback by telling participants what you have learned from them and what action you intend to take in response. (Coote, 2011:199)

She suggests that these ground rules can be adapted for businesses and other non-governmental organisations interested in sharing responsibility with their employees and/or intended beneficiaries.

Coote also addresses another problem often experienced by those seeking to develop more deliberative processes i.e. the process becomes dominated by the usual suspects and those on the margins are not really engaged. Those who are poor, vulnerable, on the margin are the most difficult to engage in these processes. Coote states:

The challenge is greater still because there are so many people in this position; they are hugely varied socially, economically, culturally and widely spread.

Experience suggests that, to achieve more equal participation, certain steps must be taken. These include:

- Identify those whose voices are seldom heard and locate them, using outreach and other community development techniques.
- Meet marginalised groups on their own territory and on their own terms, rather than trying to include token representatives in other participative exercises.
- Let marginalised groups define their own agendas and own ways of working – respect their wisdom and experience and treat them as equals.
- Share their language – literally and metaphorically.
- Consider more creative methods of communicating and working together – for example using artwork, theatre, song instead of the normal stuff of meetings.
- Invest in co=ordination and facilitation and in building and sustaining networks.
- Keep on reaching out – one-off gestures won't help.
- Feedback, reflect, learn and continue to improve ways of sharing responsibility. (ibid:200)

This is not an easy process for many people or institutions. It requires change of people and institutions.

2.8. Conclusion

There is a great need for new understandings, new approaches, new processes, new models and different outcomes if a viable, sustainable future is to emerge. The authors believe a new paradigm is required as the foundation for such developments. Deliberative democracy is another essential component and should be developed, supported and strengthened. It is essential that responsibility in shaping the future be shared. The voices and perspectives of all sectors must be heard and respected. Power differentials should be removed from this process. Decisions should be made on the basis of good analysis and viable proposals, not on the basis of the power a particular sector or group commands.

However if these changes are to occur society at large needs to understand and internalise these realities; accurate and relevant information is needed. Education is required to enable everyone to be part of these processes.

Coernilogar and Coertjens spell out some of the implications for education of a move towards greater participation and the sharing of responsibilities (Cernilogar/Coertjens, 2011). A starting point for such education could be a focus well-being and the common good. These are not universally accepted priorities yet they are essential if there is to be a sustainable future for this planet and its inhabitants. The challenges of real participation, of deliberative democracy, of intergenerational justice need to be addressed in an ongoing educational endeavour.

References

Beckert J. (2002), *Beyond the Market*, Princeton, NJ: Princeton Univ. Press.

Capra, F. (1982), *The Turning Point*, London: Fontana Books.

Capra, F. (1996), *The Web of Life*, London: HarperCollins.

Coote, A. (2011), *Equal participation: making shared social responsibility work for everyone* in Trends in Social Cohesion No. 23, (provisional version), pp. 199 -200, Strasbourg: Council of Europe.

Daly, H. E. and Cobb J.B. (1990), *For the Common Good*, London: The Merlin Press.

Denters, B. V. (2003). *The Rise of Interactive Governance and Quasi-Markets*, Den Haag: Kluwer Academic Publishers.

Dunne, J. (1991), The Catholic School and Civil Society: Exploring the Tensions in *The Catholic School in Contemporary Society*, Dublin: CMRS Education Commission.

Elster, J. (1998), *Deliberative Democracy*. Cambridge: Cambridge University Press.

Fiedler, Matthias, 2011, 'Thinking at the Fault Lines: Development as Shared Responsibility', paper presented at conference on *Rethinking Development in an Age of Scarcity and Uncertainty: New Values, Voices and Alliances for Increased Resilience*, organised by EADI: University of York, September 2011.

Flahault François , (2011), 'Conceiving the social bond and the common good through a refinement of human rights', in *Rethinking progress and ensuring a secure future for all: what we can learn from the crises.* Trends in Social Cohesion, No 22. Strasbourg: Council of Europe.

Gaudium et Spes, (1965), Vatican II Council, Maryknoll: Orbis Books, no. 4

Gopel, Maja (2011), Shared responsibilities and future generations: beyond the dominant concepts of justice' in *'Towards a Europe of shared social responsibilities: challenges and strategies*, in Trends in Social Cohesion No. 23, (provisional version), pp. 95-108, Strasbourg: Council of Europe.

Fourcade, Marion and Healy, Kieran (2007), *Moral Views of Market Society* in Annual Review of Sociology, 33, 285-311

Habermas, Jurgen (2001) *The Post-National Constellation*, Cambridge, MA: MIT

Healy, S. and Reynolds, B. (1993), 'Work, Jobs and Income: Towards a new Paradigm' in Reynolds, B. and Healy S. (eds.), *New Frontiers for Full Citizenship*, Dublin: CMRS.

Healy, S. and Reynolds, B. (2000), 'Developing Participation in a Changing Context' in Reynolds, B. and Healy S. (eds.), *Participation and Democracy: Opportunities and Challenges*, Dublin: CORI Justice Commission.

Healy, S. and Reynolds, B. (2002), 'Social Partnership after the Celtic Tiger: Challenges and Opportunities' in Reynolds, B. and Healy S. (eds.), *Choosing a Fairer Future: An Agenda for Social Partnership after the Celtic Tiger*, Dublin: CORI Justice Commission.

Healy, S. and Reynolds, B. (2005), *Securing Fairness and Well-being in a Land of Plenty*, Dublin: CORI Justice Commission.

Healy, S. and Reynolds, B. (2006), 'Progress and Public Policy: The Need for a New Paradigm' in Reynolds, B. and Healy, S. (eds.), *Progress, Values and Public Policy*, Dublin, Liffey Press, pp. 1-24

Ife, J. (2004), *Linking Community Development and Human Rights*, A paper delivered to a conference on Community Development, Human Rights and the Grassroots in Deakin University.

Hirschman, AO, (1977), Rival interpretations of market society: civilizing, destructive or feeble? J. Con. Lit. 20: 1463-84

Kuhn, T. (1970), *The Structure of Scientific Revolutions*, Chicago, University of Chicago Press.

McCabe, M. (1997), *"Clashing Paradigms: Leadership in the Church Today"*, SMA Bulletin, Christmas 1997, pp. 1-12.

National Economic and Social Council (2009), *Ireland's Five Part Crisis*, Dublin, NESC.

Offe, Claus 2011, 'Shared social responsibility: A concept in search of its political meaning and promise', Paper delivered to a conference hosted jointly by the Council of Europe and the European Commission on *Shared Social Responsibility, March 1, 2011.*

Nussbaum, Martha (2000), *Women and Human Development*, Cambridge University Press.

Rawls, John, (1971), *A Theory of Justice*, Cambridge, MA: Harvard University Press

Sacconi, Lorenzo, (2011), 'From individual responsibility to shared social responsibilities: concepts for a new paradigm', in *Towards a Europe of shared social responsibilities: challenges and strategies*, Trends in social cohesion, No 23. Council of Europe Strasbourg.

Sandel, M. 2000. What money can't buy: the moral limits of markets, in *The Tanner Lectures on Human Values*, 21:89-122, Salt Lake City: Univ. Utah Press.

Scholz, Arne (2011), 'What is commonly understood by shared social responsibility' in *Towards a Europe of shared social responsibilities: challenges and strategies*, in Trends in Social Cohesion No. 23, (provisional version), pp. 81-94, Strasbourg: Council of Europe.

Sen, Amartya (2009) *The Idea of Justice*, London: Allen Lane/Penguin

UNESCO (1997), *Declaration on the Responsibilities of the Present Generations towards Future Generations*, available at **http://www.unesco.org/cpp/uk/declarations/generations.pdf** accessed August 2011.

United Nations (1995), *Our Global Neighbourhood*, UN Commission on Global Governance was established by the United Nations Organisation. Its report published in 1995 is entitled,

Weber, M. 1958 (1904-1905). *The Protestant Ethic and the Spirit of Capitalism*, New York: Charles Scribner's Sons.

WCED, (1987), Report of the World Commission on Environment and Development: Our Common Future: From One Earth to One World, Oxford, Oxford University Press

Wuthnow, Robert (2010), *Be Very Afraid: The Cultural Response to Terror, Pandemics, Environmental Devastation, Nuclear Annihilation, and Other Threats*, Oxford: Oxford University Press.